How to be an
'Amazing Mum'
When You Just Don't
Have the Time

The ultimate
handbook for
hassled
mothers

How to be an
'Amazing Mum'
When You Just Don't
Have the Time

Tanith Carey

LION

A Lion Book
an imprint of
Lion Hudson plc
Wilkinson House, Jordan Hill Road,
Oxford OX2 8DR, England
www.lionhudson.com

ISBN 978 0 7459 5375 5

Distributed by:
Marston Book Services, PO Box 269, Abingdon, Oxon,
OX14 4YN, UK

First edition 2009
10 9 8 7 6 5 4 3 2 1 0

The text paper used in this book has been made from wood
independently certified as having come from sustainable forests.

A catalogue record for this book is available
from the British Library

Typeset in 10/13 Humanist 777 BT
Printed and bound in Great Britain by CPI Cox & Wyman, Reading

Contents

Acknowledgments

Thanks to so many mums who talked through their ideas and experiences. Special appreciation must go to Belinda Lester, Anita McBain, Tara Carey, Professor Julian Elliott, Mallory Henson, Gina Bremner, Grace Saunders, Jo Percival, Heather Holden-Brown, Simone Cave, Amanda Goodhart, Rebecca Lesser, Dinah Wilmott, Dr Nicola Lowe and Sue Harwood.

Finally, a special thank you must also go to the two people who made this book happen: Elly James, for her incredible perseverance, and Kate Kirkpatrick, for her vision.

And, of course, to my family: my daughters Lily and Clio, my husband Anthony and my own mother, Lynne, without whom this book would never have been written.

Foreword

I used to think that, as a journalist on a national newspaper, I was under a lot of pressure. When friends who'd had babies told me that it was harder work being at home looking after children than having a job, I secretly scoffed. Compared to living with the roller coaster of life in a hectic office, how hard could it be to care for one little person?

And then I had a baby.

There is no experience more relentless or all-consuming than being a mother. Like every other woman, I was utterly shocked by how little time I had to myself when I became a parent. I couldn't even go to the loo without my daughter wanting to sit on my lap. I'd tidy up the house, but as fast as I could pick up toys, she'd throw them on the floor. She'd tell me she was hungry and then didn't like what I'd cook. I'd give her everything she asked for, and she'd dream up more demands. It was, just as my friends had tried to warn me, more than a full-time job.

Like other working mums, I became like the White Rabbit in *Alice in Wonderland*. From the moment I opened my eyes in the morning, it felt as though I were in an unwinnable race against a stopwatch – constantly in a panic, always late, noticing only the time, instead of the life that was passing me by. The spare moments I did have were spent trying to cover over my under-eye bags, feeling guilty about being a poor parent – and wondering where it had all gone wrong. Morning melt-downs were a regular occurrence. It was when I looked down in horror at my coat at the school gates one morning and realized it was on inside-out that I decided there must be another way.

So I started to make a conscious effort to find ways to cut out the irritating distractions, frustrations and lost minutes that were making a hard job of being a working mother even harder. And, as I turned my mind to it, I gradually worked out ways to streamline the dozens of tasks I needed to do every day to keep the show on the road. I also spoke to other mums and experts, and tried and tested them all.

Many were just subtle changes I made to my routine as I went along, like buying products in supermarkets that were easier to use or open, or focusing on toys and activities that wouldn't need so much picking up after. Yet, even though it became obvious to me there was an epidemic of exhausted mothers out there, I was amazed to see that, despite the shelves of books telling me how to be the perfect parent, not one addressed how to find the *time* to be that person in the first place. It was then that I felt a realistic book needed to be written about what mothers need now.

This is not a book about rushing your children; nothing could be more counterproductive. Hurrying kids only makes them needier and more demanding. It's a book of short cuts that means you can spend more time concentrating on your kids, making them feel once again they are the most important people in your life. There are no complicated lists to fill out or six-week action plans to add to your already loaded to-do list. This book will show you, here and now, how you really can do everything quicker.

But don't feel it's just for working mothers. It's for any parent who just wants to spend less time tidying, cleaning and washing, and have more time to enjoy their kids. It applies just as much to the brand new mum – who can't find a moment to wash her hair – as to the company director who's struggling to get her three kids to school by 9 a.m. Some ideas will apply to your life and others won't. Dip in and out and try a few at a time. Keep this book in your handbag for the thirty seconds you snatch when the baby's asleep in the back of the car, or the ten minutes when you finally get a seat on the train home.

The reason I wrote this book is because when I brought my first baby, Lily, home I promised her that I would be an amazing mother. But, when other pressures started to steal away the hours I always meant to spend with her, I became less and less the parent I wanted to be. This book is about trying to help myself – and other mothers – reclaim that promise. You have nothing to gain but time: for your kids, your partner and, ultimately, yourself.

Part I

The Hassled Mum's Guide to Keeping Your Home – and Your Kids – Under Control in Just a Fraction of the Time

Chapter 1

End Kitchen Slavery Now...

How not to spend a second longer cooking and cleaning in your kitchen than you have to

Feeding kids healthy foods – and then cleaning up after the mess – is probably the single most time-consuming challenge for a mum-in-a-rush. But with the right equipment and a bit of forethought, there are a whole host of ways to come up with quick, fuss-free family meals that won't leave your kitchen looking like a bomb-site.

What a Busy Mum Really Needs to Get Out of the Kitchen Faster and with Less Clearing Up

The key to getting out of the kitchen quicker is to head off disasters before they happen. Imagine how much sooner you would be liberated if you didn't end up on your hands and knees at the end of every meal chipping food off the floor. Here's how to liberate yourself.

The right highchair: If your kids are still at the baby and toddler stage, you will save hours of stress simply by choosing the right highchair.
My life changed the day I traded in my quaint,

antique-style chair for an industrial-sized plastic version with a huge tray. The difference was that no matter how hard the baby tried to lob her food over the edge, the tray was now wider than her arms could stretch. Suddenly I no longer had to get down on the floor after every meal to pick up the carnage. In fact, the whole kitchen stayed cleaner because so much less food was getting traipsed around.

When looking for a highchair, check also that you can remove the tray easily – so you can dump all the debris and give it a good wipe in the sink. When your baby's first mastering finger foods, it'll save you washing up dishes and plates too.

Some of the newer models also have crumb-catcher trays, but overall, it's important the design should be simple for cleaning. Otherwise food will get wedged and cemented into all sorts of nasty nooks and crannies. If that happens, don't spend hours scrubbing it. Simply take it outside on a sunny day and wash it down with a high-pressure hose!

Floor mats and place mats: How often have you looked at the area under the kitchen table and wondered whether any of the meal you prepared was actually eaten? The amount of debris can be quite appalling, and picking it all up is one of those jobs that really makes you feel like a domestic drudge.

Make it manageable by investing in a washable plastic mat. Forget the flimsy versions you get in the baby shops. Instead, hit the web and you will find cheaper, hard-wearing ones that you can order in a range of patterns and sizes. That way you can shake out the whole mess outside or into the sink, and shove the mat in the washing machine when things get really bad. For example, at www.Happy-mats.com, you can find made-to-measure rubber-backed mats in a huge range of colours – and there's also a good range of bright designs at www.turtlemat.co.uk.

But don't stop there. Invest in some table mats as well to catch the overspill from plates. They just seem to stop the mess spreading on the table, and again, you can quickly rinse them off in the sink. Look for the wipe-clean ones that come decorated with ABCs and numbers. While waiting for her meals, my younger daughter learnt to count up to twenty!

One last point: As soon as they are out of the highchair, get children into the habit early of sitting properly and squarely at the table. It will dramatically reduce food fall-out.

The best bib: Buying the right size, shape and fabric bib is essential if you want to avoid changing your baby after almost every meal time. The most useless of all are those tiny terry towel white ones that cover about 2 inches square. Plus, you need to wash them, which only adds to your laundry mountain. Then, to add insult to injury, the Velcro snags everything in the washing machine! The other types to avoid are those ridiculous rigid bibs with the gaping necks, which leave most of your child's chest dangerously exposed.

All in all, it means the wipe-clean plastic coated ones that tie easily at the back are the most practical. For extra safety, layer them. Have a tie-around one to protect their clothes, and then put a more hard-wearing plastic pelican bib over the top to catch the falling food and save on clear-up time. The best all-in-one protection comes from the tie-on ones that cover up the sleeves, too, like a mini strait jacket. But once you find the bib that really keeps your little one clean, buy loads and keep a kitchen drawer well stocked up, so you're never tempted to start a meal without one.

The right sippy cups and glasses: Ever been greeted by an avalanche of plastic sippy cups when you opened the cupboard, and then found you didn't have a single lid that fitted any of them? As I learnt from bitter experience, like bibs, sippy cups are not an area to economize in. Find the best make and model, and stick to it from the start.

For one thing, the better ones won't drip or spill so much – so you have already headed off several disasters then and there. If you buy the same brand, you will also be able to stack them neatly so they won't cascade out of the cupboard every time you open it. Plus, you won't be unloading the entire cupboard in an infuriating search for a lid that fits – because *all* the lids will fit.

As kids get older, they won't want to be seen drinking out of sippy cups, but that doesn't mean you should allow them free rein in the rest of the house with open containers. So instead, let them choose some funky covered sports beakers in bright colours. When they have progressed to drinking out of glasses at the table, choose short, solid melamine tumblers, which hold as much as a taller glass but are less likely to be knocked over by an arm – and, even if they are, won't break.

Easy dishes: When you have kids you will probably end up using the same handful of plates and cups the whole time. Buy them in the same shape and size, so they stack easily. Keep them at the front of the cupboard in a pile for easy access. Better still, consider shallow dishes to stop kids pushing the food off and onto the table (although, as children get older, they may prefer to keep their food piles separate). Also, remember that, while it's a lovely idea to serve up food in Bunnykins bowls, most toddlers go through a phase of plate-throwing. So at the weaning stage don't bother with plates; just serve finger foods on their highchair tray. Then, when you progress to serving gooey meals, get hold of microwaveable plastic dishes with suction pads that will stick. Better still, melamine is more attractive – it looks and feels more like china – but is just as durable as plastic. Be careful, though, as it can melt in the microwave.

The Kitchen Equipment the Busy Mum Really Needs

Now you have headed off a host of meal-time disasters, here's the basic equipment you really need to make your time in the kitchen as short – and as sweet – as possible.

A big freezer: No doubt your tissue-box sized freezer compartment was just fine before you had children – and all you needed it for was a half-eaten tub of Ben and Jerry's. But now you have kids, you need something more substantial.

After all, a generously sized freezer cuts out the last minute dash to the shops you dread – with kids in tow. It also means you can cook in bulk, and you always have a meal in the fridge, however hectic your day has been.

You also won't need to be like Scott of the Antarctic and excavate through the ice to get to the fish fingers at the back. The easiest freezers to use are the upright ones with the drawers, so you can 'file' your food in the right compartment and get to what you need quickly.

A microwave: A microwave is every mum-in-a-rush's best friend, not only because it's quick, but also because it saves on endless piles of washing-up.

Now it is true that some mums are squeamish about microwaves. But even Domestic Goddess Nigella Lawson is happy to serve up microwaved bananas, mixed with warm milk, as a baby's first food. You can also use microwave bags to sterilize bottles.

There are also, of course, some adult applications. With infants demanding so much of my head space, I have lost count of the times I have forgotten to take that night's dinner out of the freezer to defrost it – only to be saved by the ping of my microwave. Don't you just hate those stringy eggy saucepans, too? Crack an egg into a microwaveable dish, and, after fifty-five seconds, you've got perfect poached egg – and no pans to clean up.

The perfect kitchen bin: Throughout this book the best test of a mother-friendly item is whether you can use it with one hand. So I recommend the bins with the one-touch flip-top lids because they are a dream to use, even with a child on your arm.

Look for a good-quality model with a generous capacity – 50 litres should do the trick – so you are not emptying it every five minutes. Also make sure it has a strong inner ring that holds securely to your black rubbish bag. Fishing it out when it has dropped to the bottom – and all the rubbish has fallen out – is no fun.

The best possible dishwasher: Not all dishwashers are made alike. This is not an item to scrimp on, because you will regret it further down the line.

If you have the space, get a large capacity one. A full dishwasher can be a serious blockage in a chaotic kitchen, so you want to be unloading it as seldom as possible. Save yourself from traipsing all over the kitchen by using the cupboards nearest your machine to store your cutlery, saucepans and china.

An easy-to-use blender: You really don't want to be messing about with lots of blades and attachments, so buy the simplest model. You can't go wrong with the jug-style type – for everything from making pureed baby food, to smoothies and, when the kids have gone to bed, cocktails!

Don't worry about washing it. Let it clean itself by filling up the jug with warm water and washing-up liquid and switching it on high for thirty seconds. When blending smaller amounts, such as baby food, a hand-held sort is easier and cheaper. Just stick it in and it will mush everything in sight – and all it needs is a quick rinse afterwards.

The dust buster: An absolute life-saver. Get the most powerful model you can buy for quick clean-ups all over the kitchen. Just detach and stick the nozzle in the dishwasher so it stays hygienic for picking up food. If you can, keep another in other areas of the house where kids tend to make a mess.

The right mops: When you are cleaning up after kids, simply choosing the right mop and floor cleaner will save you an obscene amount of time.

Don't skimp. Invest in two different types. The first is a shaggy dust mop with the widest head possible – the industrial type office cleaners use. It means you can push all the food debris into one place with just a couple of sweeps of the room. It should also have a swivelling head, so you can sweep up all the crumbs and food bits that have gathered around the edges.

Forget squeegee mops or string mops and buckets – far too much work. They leave the floor awash and need constant wringing out. Instead, use a microfibre mop. It can absorb up to seven times its own weight in fluid, and attracts dust naturally, so you don't have to use so many chemicals.

The only other thing you need is a spray bottle. Mix a strong cleaning solution with water. Keep it handy and spray sparingly, and then run over it with the microfibre mop. When the mop head gets dirty, just detach it and throw it in the washing machine. It will more than halve the time you spend cleaning the kitchen floor – and suddenly your whole kitchen will feel under control.

A Few More Things That Will Make Your Life Much Easier...

A kitchen blackboard: A big blackboard in your kitchen is an invaluable way of keeping everyone informed. Make it big enough so the whole family can reach it and write on it. Use it to keep ongoing shopping and to-do lists as well as your household rules (more of that later) and the kids' weekly activity schedules.

The one I have in my kitchen is three feet long – made out of plywood covered with blackboard paint – and even has a section for my seven-year-old's weekly spellings, so she can digest them over breakfast with her corn flakes. If you are making your own, paint it with the blackboard paint that is magnetic so you can stick up school notices too. As kids get older, make them share responsibility for keeping it up to date. So whoever uses the last spoonful of mayonnaise also has the job of adding it to the shopping list.

A milkman: Not technically a piece of equipment, but massively useful, nonetheless. Any man (or woman, no doubt) who saves you a mercy dash to the shops for milk with moaning, half-dressed children in tow is a godsend. And these days, they also deliver eggs, bread, smoothies, mineral water and even vegetables and pet food.

The latest services let you order online until 9 p.m. for early the next morning – and there is no minimum order or delivery charge. Or, you can just set up a regular order and pay by direct debit every month. Why did they ever go out of fashion?

A pantry: Avoid last-minute panics for essential staples by finding cupboard space somewhere – anywhere – in your home to use as a pantry. If you don't have the room, it doesn't have to be in the kitchen – it just has to be a cool place to store the things everyone runs out of, like loo paper, juice cartons, paper towels, washing powder, soap, cereal and canned foods. If you can keep it organized with a different shelf for each category, all the better. Stack your cans and soups of the same type on top of one another with the labels facing outwards. That way you can see how many you have and what you are running low on.

The Core Items the Busy Mum Always Needs in Her Food Cupboard

Here are a few things that won't go off quickly – and can get you out of a tight spot if you are running low.

Cream cheese: Kids love the smooth texture, and it stirs in brilliantly to make a creamy sauce for pasta. Throw in some smoked salmon for brain-boosting Omega 3.

Coconut sprinkles: Like a healthy version of hundreds and thousands, these can make a so-so dessert, like Greek yoghurt, seem exciting if you sprinkle them on top. Plus it's a sneaky way to get more fruit into kids.

Whipped cream in a can: It can be put on top of any dessert, and then sprinkled with coconut or chocolate milk powder to make any pudding look like a treat – like bananas, tinned peaches and pineapple.

Frozen yoghurt lollies: If you put anything on the end of a stick, children love it. So frozen yoghurt or smoothie lollies make a great treat – and the kids don't even realize they are good for them. Admittedly they are messy for younger kids, so get them to eat them over a bowl.

Eggs: They last safely for weeks in the fridge, and you will always be able to cook up a quick omelette or scrambled eggs.

Chorizo: It has a longer life than your average sausage and is a great fall-back to add to casseroles and to jazz up pizzas.

Long-life milk: Not ideal, obviously, but worth having a couple of cartons for those mornings when you suddenly realize you've run dry.

Rice and pasta: Without doubt, the core of a kid-friendly kitchen. At supper time, give them whole wheat versions, which have a lower glycaemic index and leave them fuller for longer. That way they won't be so hyper, will settle more easily at bedtime, and won't wake up in the middle of the night feeling hungry.

Until they are old enough, choose pasta twists and tubes over spaghetti to make it easier to eat. Admittedly, grains of rice can go everywhere and can be a nightmare to pick up afterwards. So try rice pasta, which cooks in eight minutes, looks just like regular pasta, and doesn't make such a mess.

Noodles: For a refreshing change, try noodles. Just stir in soy sauce, sweetcorn and peas.

Couscous: This is so easy, it defies belief. Simply pour some boiling water over the couscous and leave for around five minutes until it's all absorbed. Then fluff it up with a fork and add butter or vegetables, such as some tinned chickpeas.

Juice cartons: Cartons of concentrated juice often have long expiration dates and are cheaper and easy to buy in bulk because they don't need to be stored in the fridge. However, beware of giving kids too many juices made from concentrate because the sugar content is higher.

Powdered cheese: This lasts practically for ever – and though you won't win any accolades from Gordon Ramsay, the grated parmesan-style cheeses are good to have in the cupboard to add excitement to soups and pasta.

Tins: The Hurried Mum's Convenience Food

In our obsession with 'fresh' and 'organic', tinned food has long been the poor relation, considered only good for baked beans and tomato soup when the cupboard is bare. But just because canned goods are cheap and convenient doesn't mean they're unhealthy.

It's likely that since the last time you looked, food manufacturers have moved with the times. Most have cut down on the sugar and salt, and now pack fruit in its own juice, instead of sickly sweet syrups. I know I sound like a bit of a convert, but the fact is that, compared to fresh food, tinned food is cheaper and keeps longer, and it can be a life-saver when we just can't get to the shops.

Did you know that tinned fruit and vegetables often have *more* vitamins because the contents are canned when the flavour, minerals and vitamins are at their height? Compare that to fresh fruit and veg, which lose up to 50 per cent of their vitamins in the first seven days. There are fewer preservatives needed too.

Busy mums, me included, are often wary of cooking fresh fish, despite how important it is for brain development. It's got a short shelf life, can be fiddly to prepare, and, after all that work, picky kids often refuse to eat it. So for me the tinned versions win every time for ease as well as price. It's ready to use straight from the cupboard, and it's around half the cost. Be subtle, if you have to be, and stir tuna into kids' pasta sauces or use it as a sandwich filling.

Tinned fruit is also a godsend. Now it comes in pure juice, it means you can empty a tin of pineapples, peaches and strawberries into a bowl, cut them up, and have a ready-made fruit salad in about a minute – with no chopping or peeling. Canned kidney beans and chickpeas are also a fantastic source of low-cost, good-quality protein, which won't need soaking and you can use straight away in salads, stews and curries.

Tinned Goods to Always Have in Your Cupboard

Sweetcorn	Pilchards
Baked beans	Sardines
Tomato soup	Chickpeas
Tomatoes	Kidney beans
Artichoke hearts	Pineapple
Tuna	Apricots
Salmon	Peaches

Things to ALWAYS Have in Your Freezer...

Frozen fruit: Again, it won't spoil, will keep for ages, and there are lots of different uses for it. Just like lollipops, my kids love frozen fruit straight from the freezer. Blueberries, strawberries and grapes chopped in half (so they're not a choking hazard) are always big favourites. It's also great for mixing quick ice-cold smoothies, or to make porridge more fun.

Protein staples: Frozen chicken, burgers, salmon and cod are easy to cook and usually go down well with kids. With a microwave, they will only take a few minutes to thaw. Make them more exciting – and quicker to cook – by cutting them up and putting them on a stick with some chopped grilled vegetables for kebabs.

Bread and milk: Simply the basics most mums can't live without. Keep bread in the freezer and it won't go mouldy. Take out slice by slice for perfect toast in the morning – and let milk defrost in the fridge.

Fresh vegetables: We have all pulled out handfuls of wilted, forgotten vegetables from the bottom of the fridge. So leave it to your freezer instead. Again, because they have usually been frozen very quickly after harvesting, frozen veg probably often have even more vitamins than the fresh stuff, whose vitamin content will have depleted. Beans, broccoli and peas are all better frozen than tinned. Edamame – soy beans that kids can pop out of the shell like jumping beans – are always a huge hit with the fussiest

veggie-hating child, and frozen is also the best way
to buy them.

Baby food: Of course, you already know that you
can freeze a month's baby food at a time. Infants
starting solids don't need much to begin with, so
freeze in ice-cube trays. Then empty into a bag, but
label it as clearly as possible, as most baby food only
seems to come in two basic shades of orange and
green so you don't mix your peach with your carrot.
If you have older kids as well as a baby, relax a little.
Instead, just do a mashed-up, salt-free baby version of
whatever your older children eat.

Speed It Up: How to Get
Out of the Kitchen Quicker

At the end of a long day, most of us haven't got a lot of
mental energy left over to deal creatively with the 'what
to fix for dinner' problem. So draw up a meal plan for
the month ahead, full of easy main courses that you
know your kids like. Consult your kids and have fun by
pretending you are drawing up a restaurant menu.

It might take half an hour, but stick to it over the next
six months – or until boredom creeps in – and you will
be surprised by how much more in control you feel.
Plus, kids love routine and knowing what's coming next.
Everyone's on the same page, and there won't be so much
debate, because it's all been agreed up front.

Save the simplest suppers for nights that you know
will be hectic. There's something oddly comforting about
a quick plate of poached eggs every Sunday evening
when there's homework to be done and school bags to be
packed. So now you've decided what to cook, here's lots of
ways to make the cooking process even quicker.

● If you're adding vegetables to pasta, chuck them into the same saucepan for the last four minutes to save on washing-up.

● While you're cooking, put a container on the countertop to hold all your peelings, packaging and waste. That way the counter will look under control, and you won't be running back and forth to the dustbin.

● Make a hole in the middle of hamburgers. They cook faster, and the holes close up by the time they are ready.

● Grill rather than bake. It's faster and often healthier.

● If you haven't got a microwave, cook baked potatoes in an oven quicker by pushing a metal skewer through each one.

● To cook chicken in roughly half the time, pound it flat. For large cuts of meat, cut them in two.

● Take advantage of ready-made items like bagged salads. They may cost a bit more, but the time they save can make it worth it.

● When buying food, make it easier for yourself by seeking out the easiest packaging – for example, tins with ring-pull lids you can open one-handed with a baby in one arm, and flip-top ketchup bottles so you aren't chasing the lids.

● Always use foil when you're grilling. When you're a mum-in-a-rush, you don't have time to scrub off the caked-on grease. In fact, never underestimate the power of aluminium. You can line any dish, and you won't have the chore of scrubbing it afterwards.

- When you're cooking pasta or vegetables, boil the water in a kettle first because it's faster and more energy efficient.

- Make big batches of staple meals on Sunday. Then reheat them during the week. Freeze the complete meal, not just the sauce.

- Once a week, chop up the raw ingredients, grate some cheese and get the kids to build their own pizzas or tacos. Self-serve meals are massive time-savers.

More Kitchen Organization Tricks

- When you've got a lot going on, it's easy to forget even the tastiest recipe. So stick your favourites inside your kitchen cabinets, or use post-it notes to mark them in the books.

- Keep your cutlery under control. Are your dessert spoons impossible to get to under a tangle of whisks and garlic crushers? Put the specialist stuff in a different drawer so you – and hopefully your kids – can find the essentials.

- Use larger mixing bowls than you think you'll need so whatever you are blending doesn't splash or overflow. You also won't need to pour the mix into a larger bowl halfway through the preparation either.

- Keep a sink filled with soapy water to rinse utensils and soak pots as you go. It's especially important with breakfast bowls, spattered with rice crispies or corn flakes. Left out all day, they can harden to the consistency of concrete.

29

● Wipe spills off the hob as soon as they happen, before they dry rock-hard. To stop spilled food making black marks, pour salt onto the spillage.

● Take two minutes to throw out all the old food and give the fridge a wipe just before you get your new shopping in. Throw away the chocolate sauce or whatever other condiments you have had lurking at the back of the freezer since you moved in. After two years, I guarantee you will never ever feel like eating them. Try to put the food with pending expiration dates at the front so it doesn't get forgotten.

● Only stock your fridge with nutritious snacks that you are happy for your older children to eat. Keep them at their level at the front of the fridge, so they can help themselves with your permission. Just make it a condition that they don't take food out of the kitchen – to avoid cheese triangles trodden into the shag-pile – and that they throw all the packaging away.

● Make the most of your worktop space by keeping out only appliances you use every day. Toasters and microwaves are useful. Juicers, which get used twice a year on the first day of your health-kick, and coffee makers only used for dinner parties, are not. Put the stuff you use most at eye-level so you can reach it the most easily and it feels accessible. Use wall space to get things off the surfaces by buying magnetic knife holders and hanging spice racks.

● Appalled by the amount of grease that builds up on the tops of your kitchen cupboards and your fridge? Head off the heinous job of wiping it off by cutting grease-proof paper to size and putting it on top. Then, rather than having to swab off all the muck yourself, remove and replace the paper.

● Resist the temptation to rip open the tops off of plastic food packaging, like rice and pasta. Inevitably you will create a gaping hole that will spill out the contents into your kitchen cupboards, which will then look depressingly slovenly. Instead, use a pair of kitchen scissors to snip off the top corner – and delight in cupboards not littered with old pasta spirals, sunflower seeds, popcorn kernels and the rest.

● In the summer, reduce your floor and surface cleaning time – and have more fun – by suggesting the kids eat outside and have a picnic.

● Cook meals for the kids – like chilli or casserole – that, with a bit of spicing up, would double as a meal for you and your partner when the children are in bed.

The Equipment You Need to Get Out of the Kitchen Quicker

A well-designed toaster: A toaster is key to the smooth running of your breakfast time, so choose carefully. Look for a more expensive one with an easily removable tray so it doesn't spew a never-ending fountain of breadcrumbs over your countertops. Also check that the toaster pops up the toast, rather than leaving you to singe your fingers – or worse still, use a fork – to fish it out. Also save the time and bother of using your oven grill by getting a toaster with slots wide enough to toast thicker items like crumpets, buns and bagels.

Sharp knives: Nothing is more frustrating or time-wasting than a blunt one.

A pair of scissors: Absolutely the quickest way to cut up ham and countless other types of meat – and once you've used it to slice up pizza, you'll never use one of those rolling pizza slicers again. Have them on hand to cut up herbs, slice the stems off flowers and open packaging.

A quality tin-opener: They do wear out, and if you're struggling to open a tin for a second longer than you need to, bin it and get one that does the job smoothly without making jagged edges.

An easy-to-use kitchen timer: When you've got demanding children in the background, it's easy to take your eye off the ball – and boiling pan – with messy consequences.

A decent spatula: Save your fingers – and trying to dangle hot food precariously from forks – and invest in a couple of good-sized spatulas for lifting off fish fingers, burgers, sausages and pizza.

Decent saucepans: Good-quality pans will cook better and more evenly and are less likely to scorch food. Make sure they have got heat-resistant handles so they can go in the oven, and so you don't need to find an oven glove to take them off the stove.

Five-Minute Meals: Healthy and Nutritious Meals That *Really Do* Take Just Five Minutes to Prepare

Pitta bread pizza: Don't faff about waiting for the pizza dough to cook. Instead, pop a piece of pitta bread in the toaster to warm both sides, and while it's doing that, turn the grill on. Then cover one side with tomato paste, cheese and other toppings like tuna, mushrooms or sausage – and heat.

Scrambled egg and smoked salmon: With wholemeal bread and Omega 3-packed quality protein, this is pretty much the perfect meal.

Chops and sausages: Just grill in minutes with some foil at the bottom of the tray for the feeling you are giving your kids a real meat supper.

Tomato soup with cheesy bits and whole-wheat toast: Don't feel guilty about serving soup. It can be a power food, and there are lots of ways to make sure it's packed with protein. Pea and ham, lentil and ham, and chowders are all great meals in themselves. Even a bog-standard can of Heinz Cream of Tomato soup is 84 per cent tomatoes, and can become a complete meal with some cheddar cheese cubes thrown in, served with some brown bread and butter soldiers. Do keep an eye on the salt content, though, as it can be high in some tinned versions.

Cod and veg: Just chuck a cod piece in a saucepan with some frozen peas and carrots, some milk and butter – and you have another wholesome meal.

Roast chicken drumsticks: Cheat by buying roast chicken drumsticks, and then pop them under the grill to make them tender and sizzling, as if you'd cooked them from scratch yourself.

Pasta with cheesy tomato sauce and veg: Throw frozen broccoli and sweetcorn into the cooking pasta. Then drain and stir in some tomato paste and cheddar cheese to make it gooey – and it's done. Another variation is to stir in cream cheese with ham or smoked salmon for protein.

A Word on Cereals...

On evenings when you are late home or the kids are tired, you won't kill them by giving them a bowl of cereal. These days most are nutritionally fortified – and don't forget that muesli was originally designed as the perfect food. Buy the bite-sized versions and the brands without sugar. Give preference to oat-based kinds like mini Oatibix, which are easier to eat, will keep kids feeling fuller for longer and are quicker than porridge.

No-cook Dishes That are Just as Healthy

For some reason, many of us feel we are not being good mothers if we are not preparing our children a hot meal every day. While there is something comforting about that idea, let yourself off the hook. Food that's raw often has more nutrients and can be just as satisfying – and even more varied than cooked food. Try these.

Kids' ploughman's lunches: This is fun for your kids to eat, and there's no washing-up afterwards. Try oatcakes, hummus, cold chicken drumsticks, cheese strings, salami and halved cherry tomatoes. Just make sure there's a good selection of protein, whole carbs and vegetables.

Crunchy raw vegetables: Don't feel you always have to cook vegetables. Kids actually prefer something to crunch. As a side order at meals, present them manageable little ramekin dishes of carrot sticks, crispy runner beans, multicoloured peppers or halved cherry tomatoes.

Kebabs: Kids love anything on a stick. Try halved cherry tomatoes and little rounds of mozzarella. You can also try making them with fruit – cubes of melon and kiwi look gorgeous. In fact, if you cut anything into bite-sized pieces and arrange them in some sort of order, they look more appetizing. For younger kids, use wooden sticks and snap the points off when you serve.

A Word on Breastfeeding and Weaning

It's not always as easy as it should be, but if you have the knack and you enjoy it, keep breastfeeding – not only because it's good for your child, but because it will save you hours sterilizing bottles, mixing formula and the rest. Some mums will say it's quicker to feed your baby with a bottle and you can leave them to it after a certain age, but I still think overall it's more flexible and convenient to have it on tap.

If you are at the weaning stage, you can also make your life easier when you go out by packing vacuum-packed squeezable fruit smoothies and baby foods. Brands like Ella's are just pureed fruit and veg, but they come in handy squishy packs. It means you can either squeeze the contents into a spoon, or because they have baby-safe openings, just give them to your infant to suck straight from the packet. Brilliant.

The Busy Mum's One-Stop Guide to One-Pot Cooking

When you cook, remember that a healthy home-cooked family meal doesn't have to use every piece of cookware in your kitchen or take hours to clean up afterwards. Instead, go for one-pot recipes, where you can put all the ingredients into a single dish and let them stew together. Better still, invest in a slow cooker or 'crock pot'. They are electrically powered to cook at low temperatures over longer periods. That way you could throw a few things in the pot in the morning, leave it with no risk of burning, and have a hot meal ready to serve for supper. They are especially good for casseroles or dishes containing meat like chicken and lamb. You can also throw in vegetables, pasta and rice. For example, try pouring a tin of mushroom soup over chicken with carrots and potatoes in the morning and leave it on a low heat. You won't even have to look at it again until it's ready to dish up in the evening.

The Busy Mum's Guide to Getting Fruit and Veg into the Kids without an Argument:

When you are a mum-in-a-rush, you don't have a lot of time for rows. But what happens when the issue is something as important as eating fruit and veg – and your kids refuse point blank to eat their five-a-day? Here are some quick and easy ways of packing kids full of fruit and veg without them even realizing it.

Dip them: Make it fun for kids by giving them dips to dunk their veggies in. Try hummus, soft cheese or guacamole. They'll be more interested in dipping than the fact they are eating something that's good for them.

Spread them: Try nut butters instead of butter or margarine to get more good fats into your child's diet. As well as peanut butter, you can also try hazelnut and cashew nut butter from health food shops.

Mini-size them: Make small portions more appetizing by presenting them in ramekin dishes. Choose mini veg, too. Baby plum tomatoes, sweetcorn and carrots are always favourites because they just look so cute.

Pop them: Let your kids pop the beans out of edamame or out of peapods. The end result will be too tempting to resist.

Blend them: Make soups by steaming lots of vegetables until soft, then add boiling water and blend into a smooth puree. Broccoli, cauliflower, carrots, parsnips, swede, spinach, tomatoes, squash, sweet potatoes and celery can all be thrown in – and by the time it's come out of the mixer, kids won't have a clue what went into it. All they'll know is that it's a cool colour.

Experiment with smoothies: Kids love throwing different types of fruit in the blender, pressing the button and seeing what shade it comes out as. Try bananas, mangoes, pineapples, papayas, peaches, nectarines, pears and all the different berries. You can also put all the ingredients into the mixing jug the night before, add the juice or milk, refrigerate, and all you have to do the next morning is press the 'on' button to have the perfect ice-cold smoothie for breakfast. Throw in some nuts, oat flakes or plain yoghurt to make it more substantial.

Let them make pizza: Buy some dough bases – or again use pitta bread – and let kids create funny faces and patterns using halved baby tomatoes, sweetcorn and red peppers. They will be more likely to gobble up half a tomato if it's the nose on the clown they have made.

Get sneaky: When my children sit down to watch a DVD, I take advantage of the fact that they are distracted by planting a little bowl of fruit or veg in front of them. They will absentmindedly eat anything – try carrot sticks, halved grapes, blueberries or raisins. When they are starving and waiting for dinner, also keep them busy with strips of crispy vegetables until their main meal is ready.

Compartmentalize: For younger kids, use an ice-cube tray and put bite-sized portions of colourful fruit and veg in each compartment. Call them comedy names to make them seem more fun, like apple smiles, carrot light sabres, and kiwi cartwheels. If you feel your kids aren't eating enough good foods at main meals, let them snack from the tray all day if they want to. They're more likely to eat from it because it feels like their idea.

How to Deal with Time-Consuming Picky Eating

When you're up to your eyes, you don't have time to deal with fussy eating. At meal times, anything your child is going to eat will probably be gobbled up in the first fifteen minutes. After that, they've most likely lost interest, and you're wasting your time. Pushing a loaded-up spoonful of food into a child's face will just put them off even more and will turn meal times into a power struggle. Your child will always win, because at the end of the day, it's their mouth, and they know very well that it's ultimately up to them whether they open it or not.

So don't make it into a drama, or waste more time trying to serve up another meal. Instead quietly offer them a piece of bread and cheese with a slice of fruit and a glass of milk, or a bowl of cereal with some fruit juice. They will realize that moaning isn't getting them anywhere, get bored and hopefully eat more at their next meal.

Do respect the fact that your children will have definite likes and dislikes. Often they are just born with different palates. My youngest child would eat broccoli for Britain. My eldest physically gags at the taste of it, but she can't eat enough blueberries and strawberries, so it all evens out. Luckily there is enough variety on the shelves for parents to find something their kids will like. Remember that it takes kids up to fifteen tries of a new food before they get used to it. So keep feeding them off your plate, and they will soon develop their own favourites.

Fast Lunch Boxes

If your child's school has school meals, take them with both hands. Now that Jamie Oliver has performed his magic, hopefully the mouth-watering selection on offer should save you the hassle. However, there are mums who have no choice, and for them, it's a nightly chore. The ideal packed lunch should contain protein, whole grains, dairy products, fruit and vegetables. A tall order, but with a few short cuts, it can be done in a matter of minutes.

● Freeze Marmite sandwiches in bulk. Cut up a whole loaf and put each round of sandwiches in a freezer bag. Take them out in the morning. By the time it's lunch they will have defrosted. The same can be done with muffins.

● Cut down the time you spend buttering, slicing and cutting the crusts off bread. Roll instead. Buy tortillas and spread them with cream cheese so they stick. You can also buy crustless bread – or simply tell your child not to be so fussy!

● Use pitta pockets. Just cut out a small hole and stuff with your child's favourite things like cheese sticks or slices.

● Boil some extra pasta at dinnertime. Stir in pesto and sweetcorn with the leftovers, and store in a plastic container for lunch for the next two days.

● Skip the irritation of spreading too-hard butter – and making gaping holes in the bread – by just using peanut butter.

● Leave out the bread completely. Instead, use a thin deli slice of ham or turkey on top of a slice of cheese and roll them up. Cut in half and wrap them in foil. Or try it with salami. Spread with cream cheese.

● Stick a piece of pitta bread in for your child to tear up and dip into mini pots of hummus.

● Use the leftovers from dinner the night before. Save a chicken drumstick and pack with a frozen juice drink to keep cold. Cold pizza is delicious as an occasional treat, and no less nutritious than a cheese sandwich, if more fat-laden. Sausages are also delicious cold.

● From the age of eight, make preparing packed lunches your child's responsibility. Try it just two or three days a week at first so it feels like a treat. Ask them to do it while you make the supper, so all the mess is over and done with in one go. Lay out the breakfast bowls and cups at the same time.

Healthy Take-Away Options on Nights When You Can't Face Cooking

If you choose carefully, take-aways don't have to be unhealthy. For the occasional night when you just don't have time, let alone the energy, to cook, keep the menus in your kitchen or office drawer as a special treat for you and the kids when you get home.

Fish and chips: Make sure kids don't just gorge themselves on the batter and check that they eat the flesh too. When it comes to chips, the thicker the better – they absorb less fat.

Italian: With pizza, stay away from high-fat cheese-filled crusts and pepperoni and garlic bread. Instead, pile on the tomatoes, mushrooms, sweetcorn and olives and take advantage of salad side dishes often on offer. Rather than just plain pasta, order raviolis filled with vegetables.

Indian: The good news is that Indian food is packed full of vegetables. Just choose the milder dishes cooked in tomato-based sauces rather than the deep-fried extras like samosas and pakoras. Look for veggie and lentil side dishes.

Chinese: Opt for stir-fried and steamed, not deep-fried, dishes. Choose boiled and egg-fried instead of deep-fried rice. Kids may love them, but don't let them fill up completely on prawn crackers. A healthier option would be Thai food, which is more likely to be made up of steamed rice, fish and veg. And of course, if you can get your kids to develop a taste for it, try sushi. They can fall in love with the bite-sized bundles of flavour, chopsticks and presentation trays. If you are worried about the raw fish, choose the veggie option, and order a plate of edamame – soy popping beans – to go with it.

Supermarket Shopping: How to Never Again Face the Shops with a Screaming Child in Tow

Why any woman would voluntarily brave the supermarket with children in tow is a mystery to me. With younger kids, it's like a bad version of *Supermarket Sweep* – only with a ticking time-bomb in the front of your trolley.

Temptation everywhere – and an audience of hundreds if it all blows up in your face. Avoid it where possible and use a home-delivery shopping service.

- If your internet connection is sluggish, upgrade your broadband and you could do your entire grocery shopping for the week in ten minutes by pretty much repeating last week's order.

- Get wireless internet, and with a laptop you will be able to order your groceries from anywhere in the house when you can snatch a spare few minutes.

- Shop around for the fastest and easiest supermarket site. Make sure they give small delivery slots so you aren't left hanging around with impatient kids waiting for the shopping to show up.

- Consider choosing one of the late night delivery times so you can give your fridge a wipe and unpack the groceries when the children are in bed. At some of the big supermarkets, evening delivery slots are marginally cheaper too.

- Give preference to a delivery service which carefully sorts out your products into different coloured bags like frozen goods and toiletries – so you can unpack them faster. You're paying for convenience after all.

- Keep an ongoing grocery list on a notice board in the kitchen so you don't waste time reaching back into the inner recesses of your brain to remember what you need. Or keep a list on your mobile phone and add to it as and when you think of something. It's probably the one object you have on your person at all times.

● When choosing a supermarket delivery service, find a company that will bring your food slap-bang into your kitchen – not, as has happened to me, send a delivery man who refused to cross the threshold, citing health and safety. He then dumped fifteen bags on the doorstep for me to haul in with a hysterical baby in my arms. The kitchen was four feet in front of him. Not surprisingly, I switched supermarkets.

● Involve the kids. If your children won't give you a minute to get to the computer, let them help. Now that websites have little pictures of the foods on offer, it can be fun – and even a learning process for a child just learning fruit and veg names or the meaning of pounds and pence.

And When You Just Can't Avoid It...

Of course, even with the best will in the world, no mum is ever going to manage to avoid going to the supermarket completely. So if you really have to go, keep your head down, armed with these tips.

● Go at the quietest times – like mid-morning. At least with young children, you are likely to be up, dressed and ready to shop earlier than the rest of the adult population.

● Make the deli counter your first port of call, and pick up free samples of cheese or other snacks to keep kids happy on the way around.

● Get kids to imagine their own shopping lists, and ask them to look for those items as you go around.

● Make shopping fun by going to markets at weekends. Kids are bound to get offered free

samples at farmer's markets too. Give them a
pound to choose what they would like to buy.

And if You Really Have Nothing Left to Eat in the House...

Smile and make a virtue of it. For older kids, make
a tapas supper by warming up leftovers and serving
them in ramekin dishes.

Chapter 2

Not Another Piece of Lego...

How to spend less time on your hands and knees picking up playthings – and choosing toys that make less mess

Toys, toys, toys. One minute you've started out with a baby rattle and a couple of cuddly animals. The next minute you're knee deep in the casts of *In the Night Garden* and *Harry Potter*.

Next to cleaning the kitchen and doing the laundry, there is nothing quite like the endless task of picking up playthings to grind a harassed mum down. There have been times when I have literally gasped in horror at the thick lava of puzzle pieces, blocks, dried-out play dough bits, doll's house furniture and discarded books that has spread through my house. But by weeding out the messiest toys – and making sure what's left is organized – there really are ways to reduce your workload.

How to Head Off Kids' Mess Before It Starts

● Many mums are drowning in bits and pieces because their kids simply have too much. The average child gets around seventy new toys a year. So it's inevitable that if you don't have a clear-out, it will quickly become unmanageable. Try the 'one in, one out' rule. A few times a year, ask them what toys they don't like. Suggest they take them to a charity shop so they learn about giving.

● When kids are older, motivate them by letting them eBay stuff they no longer want – and then let them use the money to redecorate their rooms. Suggest grandparents and relatives give their time – or theatre tickets or fun experiences – rather than gifts.

● Think before you buy. Consider how much space a new toy will take up and how long the novelty will last. Toys with flashing lights or whirring noises will also need a steady flow of battery changes, so steer clear of the extra work. Certainly avoid battery-operated toys with panels that need to be removed with a screwdriver. How much time do these manufacturers think you have?

● Don't forget that the old-fashioned basics are still the best. A ball, a skipping rope, pencils and some paper will be cheaper, take up less room and encourage your kids to be more creative. Don't panic that your kids are losing out on vital educational opportunities because they haven't got the latest all-singing, all-dancing learning game. Remember that all Newton needed was a tree and an apple.

● Get good containers for pencils, felt tips and crayons. Don't you just hate those flimsy, floppy plastic wallets that so many felt tips come in? The only way to tidy them away is to slot them in one by one! Cardboard containers will also become dog-eared quickly, leaving you to scrabble around on the floor when all the crayons fall out of the bottom. You'd be better off decanting them into a good-quality shoebox, cutlery divider or even zip-lock bags. Also fantastic are professional make-up artists' silver boxes with drawers that unfold. It's like a carry-around craft case.

- Don't let children get into the habit of pulling everything off the shelves – for you to put back. From the age of three, introduce a rule that they can get a maximum of only three games or books out at a time. If they want to play with more, they need to return the ones they've used to the proper place.

- Younger children concentrate better when they have just a few good toys instead of too much choice. Keep extra items in boxes marked 'Toys on Holiday', and rotate them. You'll end up doing a lot less tidying.

- Put danger toys out of sight. Keep messy toys that need adult supervision up and out of the way to avoid disaster. Otherwise you risk felt-tip art on your sofa and play-dough cement between your floorboards.

- Adults, let alone kids, have a hard time controlling gloopy glue. It either doesn't come out at all or splurges out all over the table. Where possible use glue sticks instead. Get a lot of economy-priced ones. It's true that they need their lids, but if they dry up, just cut the tops off to reveal the fresh stuff underneath.

- The words 'Can I do some painting?' bring many a mum out in a cold sweat. If it's a fine, windless day, let them do it outside where the mess won't matter so much. Get an old wallpaper roll, weigh or tape it down, and let them go for it. If you just can't face painting at home, take advantage of craft sessions at your local library. They are usually free, and best of all, the tidy-up is someone else's responsibility.

● Set up a notice board for displaying your child's best drawings, but try to limit the display to ones that show particular flair or are developmental milestones. If your notice board is magnetic, make sure you get the most powerful magnets you can buy, so they are not constantly dropping off. When the notice board is full, edit the pictures down and put the best into a plastic A3 folder.

● The same applies to kids' 3-D creations, which quickly take up a huge amount of play space. As much as I love my daughter's art, my heart has sometimes sunk at the sight of paper mache masks, cereal box models and Easter bonnets she has brought home from school. So after a respectable amount of time, take a picture of your child posing with their work of art as a keepsake, and then ask if it's OK to make room for their new art projects.

● For older kids, invest in a jigsaw mat so they can roll up and put away half-finished puzzles, instead of leaving them hanging around taking up space. On the same subject, avoid those kids puzzle books that have a jigsaw per page. They seem like good value at the time, but pieces persistently tumble out, and you'll have no choice but to find the right page and place each time.

Toys to Avoid Until Your Child is Old Enough

Many parents secretly like to think their child is quite advanced for their age. But there are often good developmental reasons why certain toys are only recommended for certain age groups, not least of which is because they are not grown up enough to know how to put them away afterwards.

No one wants to deprive their child of a vital developmental opportunity. But the fact is that if you are too terrified to get out the messiest games – because you can't face the endless fiddly pieces – kids won't play with them anyway.

Here are some of the messiest toys – and alternatives that don't take so much tidying up after.

SWAP: Beads for Lacing Kits

For learning hand and eye coordination, lacing kits – where your child threads a string through a wooden picture – are just as good and not nearly as fiddly to tidy up afterwards as beads.

SWAP: Felt Tips for Crayons or Doodle Boards

Until kids are about six, they generally don't put felt-tip lids back on. This leaves you to do it, as well as dumping you with the task of weeding out the dead ones which have all dried up. Plus, an uncapped felt tip can cause horrible damage to walls, furniture and upholstery.

Crayons are generally easier. But save the packs of 100, containing every colour under the sun, until kids really do care about the difference between puce and blush pink. For younger kids, a set of no more than about twelve is quite enough for their drawings – and of course, as with felt tips, make sure they are the washable sort. Limiting the number of colours will mean you won't have to chase so many around the house.

With toddlers who are just learning to scribble, you can also save yourself clean-up time by giving them an all-in-one wipe-clean doodle board with a stylus attached. Of course, you will want your child to have something to show for his effort by giving him some paper. But a wipe-clean doodle board is perfect for just putting in the practice.

Another quick word of warning: beware of art projects for which you can only use the special pens provided – because, guess what, after day one the pens will get lost or dry up, and the item will hang around being completely useless and getting on your nerves!

SWAP: Poster Paints for Watercolours – Use Aqua Paints

I hate poster paints: they are horrible to pour out, splatter everywhere and then dry up. As soon as your child is old enough, basic watercolours are a much less heavy-handed approach and make a tenth of the mess. If your kids really are splashy Jackson Pollocks, save yourself some clean-up time by buying Aquadraw mini mats. All kids need to do is fill the pen or brush with a bit of water, then draw on the mat to reveal the picture. Because they're painting with water, there's no chance of staining.

SWAP: Lego for Duplo or Wooden Blocks

Kids don't really know how to apply the right sort of pressure to build Lego until they are about four, and as the pieces seem to get smaller all the time, they can be a nightmare to clean up after – and even more painful to step on. Until your children are ready, try larger-sized Duplo or wooden blocks, which are easier to fit together – and also to clear up.

SWAP: Flash Cards for Flip Books

If you're intent on making your infant a baby Einstein or want to quiz your primary-aged kids on multiplication, don't buy the loose flashcards, which can easily spill out and spread. Instead opt for the flip-book versions. They are just as good but usually spiral-bound with the question on one side and the answer on the other.

SWAP: Magnetic Toys for Fuzzy Felt

You might assume a magnet is a magnet, but actually they vary in strength wildly. You may well find that when you buy magnetic books and games, the pictures, letters or numbers are not as sticky as you might have hoped, and all the pieces are constantly dropping out. Fuzzy felt does the same job – and stays put better.

SWAP: Playworlds for Fold-away Book Versions

Rather than let a plastic or wooden model toy castle or fairyland take over your living room, buy the fold-away 3-D books. They are large paper versions of farms, palaces, castles and pirate ships that can just be closed up in an instant with the characters inside and put away neatly on the bookshelf.

SWAP: Board Games for Online Versions

On the days you can't face picking up stray Scrabble letters, chess pieces and Monopoly money – and are also fed up with tip-toeing around unfinished board games – let your older kids play them online. There are fantastic, realistic versions easily available free on your computer – even Snakes and Ladders.

SWAP: Glitter for Glitter Glue Pens

We all love glitter, but as a parent, I have discovered that only sand is as insidious and hard to get rid of.

I am embarrassed to say I once found it in my baby's nappy. Let kids use the loose stuff at school or at the library. At home, stick strictly to glitter glue pens.

SWAP: Battery-operated Toys for Wind-up Toys

It seems that whenever I have bought something battery operated for my children, within three months it's lying in a corner gathering dust – waiting for me to organize a battery amnesty. Go the old-fashioned route and buy wind-up toys instead. They are usually nicer anyway. Just don't buy the ones with the removable keys or they will inevitably get lost, and also render them useless.

How to Get Toys Organized

Now you've hopefully pared it back to the basics, find a place for everything. It will not only speed up your tidying time – it will also enable your kids to help tidy up.

- Set up small toy storage areas for younger kids throughout the house so they can play close to wherever you are, and there is always somewhere to put their games in a hurry.

- Put hooks at children's level to get stuff out of the way. Have a look at how a nursery school is set up. For example, try hanging coat pegs at child height in the hallway to stop your children chucking coats on the floor. Hang more hooks in their play areas to hold aprons, dress-up clothes or anything that could get crumpled if it's stuffed away.

- My test of good storage is whether you can throw in toys (the non-breakable kind obviously!) from about six feet across the room. Have boxes large enough – ideally about a foot long – but not so huge that they become bottomless pits.

● Also look for containers on wheels that can be rolled out for tidying and, if necessary, can be wheeled right to the heart of the worst mess, then pushed back against the wall or behind the sofa.

● It's a crime not to use the storage space under kids' beds, so invest in shallow plastic boxes, again on wheels, so kids can easily roll them in and out.

● Label boxes. There's no point having everything beautifully stored if you have to pull it all out to identify what's what. Label with simple words or if your kids can't read, pictures of what's inside. It means even the littlest children can find what they want and, crucially, help put it away again. Don't waste time trying to peel off old labels. Instead, just stick new labels over the old ones, or if you're really determined to get them off, use warm soapy water.

● Build open, secure low shelves in the alcoves of your child's room; they store much more than ready-made units. Kids can get what they want and put it back, and there's no risk of them toppling over.

● In the sitting room, invest in a toy box that fits into your décor, so it can be quickly reclaimed as an adult space the moment that the kids are in bed. Sea-grass or wicker baskets are unobtrusive and lightweight to open, and there's less risk of a heavy lid banging down on little fingers or heads. For safety, get a box with a support to hold the lid open.

How to Get the Kids to Help Tidy

● Don't be a slave to your children. Experts say that when kids do things for themselves, it builds self-esteem. Remember that by the time children are five, they are able to pick up clothes, put dirty ones in the laundry, straighten duvets, help set and clear the table and put away their toys.

● A young child in full flow can create a new mess every minute. So harness that natural energy with some reverse psychology, and make tidying up a game. It may not work perfectly, but at least you will feel as though it's all getting slightly better, not worse! Let them enjoy making a noise as they drop the blocks back into the box. Buy a mini shopping trolley and suggest they go 'shopping' for toys.

● When you're tidying, give kids a running commentary on what you are doing. As you put things back, explain: 'Your books go on your bookcase.' Putting it into words will reinforce the message. Make the process more imaginative by transforming the container where they store their Polly Pockets into 'Polly Pocket World', or *Pirates of the Caribbean* figures into a desert island.

● With older kids, challenge them to a 'ten-second tidy' so it doesn't feel like such a chore. Crank up the music to get the energy going. If the dust is starting to form a thick coat around their rooms, give kids a pair of old socks and challenge them to see who can collect the most dirt.

● Emphasize that your family is a team, and that everyone is responsible for keeping your home pleasant to live in. Make them see the advantages by explaining that it helps them to find their toys.

● Schedule clean-up time at the same time every day so kids get into the habit – usually the interval just before supper. Choose the ten minutes before their favourite TV programme to get them focused.

● Improve the chances of getting everything in the right place by equipping each bedroom with generous-sized rubbish and laundry bins. Tell older kids that only the clothes that make it to a laundry basket will get washed. Make it ritual for them to empty it into the main laundry bin at least once a week.

● At the end of the day, get your kids to pick up every toy they see. The first game of the next day will be sorting them out again. Keep a general knick-knack drawer as a holding pen for one-off puzzle pieces and bits of Lego until you have time to return them to their proper homes.

● Teach older kids the consequences of leaving a mess. Give a warning, then collect and keep anything you find on the floor. It only takes confiscating an i-Pod once for a kid to get the point.

● Don't expect perfection. At the end of the day, with children you need a family home – not a show house.

A Note on Television

Few mums feel good about putting kids in front of the TV.
But let's face it, it's one of the few kinds of entertainment
that doesn't make any mess – and saves your sanity when
you're really up against it. The experts' golden rule seems
to be that TV should never be allowed to replace active
play, exercise or socializing with children their own
age. I quite agree, but when a gentle, nurturing piece of
television steps in to replace bad tempers, sibling scraps
and a mummy melt-down, I'm all for it!

Nevertheless, some of my worst cases of motherhood
guilt have been when I have rolled out *The Lion
King* or *Shrek* as a baby-sitter (although I obviously
felt considerably better about anything starring Julie
Andrews).

But the fact is that there are times when kids need to
veg out too, and as long as it's not a regular daily diet,
it can bring the world to life in a way that even the best
books never can. There is probably not a school in the
country that doesn't use TV as an occasional teaching tool.

Play it safe by treating screen time as a special treat –
and keeping it under control by buying DVDs and sticking
to channels you feel will teach them something. Here's
how to make TV work for you.

> ● There have been times in my life when, for the
> sake of some peace and quiet, I simply couldn't
> get to CBeebies quickly enough, only to find
> I had to scroll through 104 cable channels
> – including eight ads for porn pay-per-view
> stations – to get there. Key CBeebies, Nick Jr and
> Milkshake into your remote control favourites
> list for emergencies. That way you can speed
> dial through them quicker in times of dire need,
> without exposing your kids to anything you'd
> rather they didn't see.

● Of course, we can't control everything kids are exposed to – but it's worth a try. So to that end, try not to introduce pointless, loud cartoons, which are the TV equivalent of junk food. Make yourself feel better by steering them towards educational programmes. Up to a certain age, say about seven, they don't know any different. As long as it's TV, they're happy.

● Studies have shown that repeated showing of educational videos can reinforce some learning in young children. So letting them watch their favourite programme, but within reason, is not such a bad idea after all. They will also learn more if you talk them through it; first sit down and explain it.

● Head off rows over programmes you don't want your kids to watch – but they already know about – by getting in touch with your cable company and blocking channels. As one of my mother friends said: 'We just told my five-year-old son that Horrid Henry wasn't coming to our house any more.'

● If you are tired of the constant hunt for the numerous remote controls, use Velcro to stick them to the side of the TV.

● Look for DVDs that encourage responses from children so they do not sit there watching passively. For example, the 'Eyewitness' series covers a long list of subjects from science and nature and has interactive features.

Virtually Guilt-free TV/DVD Choices

Most of these programmes are not regularly on TV, so your best bet is to get the DVD

Anything from the 'Baby Einstein'/'Bright Baby'/'Baby Genius' series

Spot's Alphabet and *Spot Learns to Count*

Winnie the Pooh ABC's and 123's

The 'Eyewitness' series

First Fun with Spanish/French

The 'Horrible Histories' series

Life on Earth, *The Living Planet* or anything with David Attenborough

Letterland

'The Magic Key' series

The 'Jolly Phonics' series

The 'Numberjacks' series

'The Way Things Work' series

Chapter 3

Time to Get Dressed...

How to dress your kids in less time and get out of the house quicker

When buying clothing for kids, don't just choose clothes on the basis of how they look. For your own sake, it's essential that their wardrobe also needs to be easy to put on, easy to coordinate and easy to launder. So by all means dress your children beautifully, but at the same time select clothes that make your life a little less complicated.

How to Dress Your Kids in Half the Time, without the Fuss...

- Before you buy, consider how easy a garment will be to put on your child. Clothes with fiddly buttons or zips should be for special occasions only. Instead, look for poppers, which are much less hassle to fasten. Elastic waistbands are super convenient, or look for elasticated materials that can be stretched over the head.

- Never buy an outfit that looks remotely creased. If it looks ruffled in the shop, how do you think it will look when you get it home?

● The average one-year-old needs up to five outfit changes a day. So look for reversible baby and toddler clothes. Another trick is to dress them in a few light layers. Every time they dirty their top layer, peel it off to reveal a fresh one underneath.

● Buy clothes that do two jobs: coats with hoods for babies so you don't lose hats, and all-in-one body suits so you don't have to worry about socks.

● Check neck openings. Nobody enjoys the struggling and screaming that ensues when you can't get a top over a baby's or toddler's head. So look for boat necks or tops with poppers on the shoulders. Steer very clear of polo and turtle necks.

● Make it fun – sing a song of 'Pop Goes the Weasel' as your child's head comes through the other side to press home the idea that they'll only be in the dark for an instant. If your child really hates pullovers being yanked down over his head, try cardigans until the phase passes.

● Choose clothes with clues. Buy socks with fitted heels so both you – and later your child – will put them on the right way around. Look for underwear that has a picture on the front to help kids identify which way around it goes.

● Until kids are about five, choose shorter, three-quarter-length sleeves so their cuffs don't get dirty or need to be constantly rolled up when they wash their hands.

● When it comes to outdoor gear, cut down the time you spend zipping and buttoning up coats. Buy poncho or cagoule styles for kids that you can throw on over anything they are wearing and still keeps them warm.

● Buy socks in only one colour and style. Harassed mums don't have the time to search for the only other matching colour at the bottom of the sock drawer. If you only buy white from the beginning, most socks will go together, more or less. Buy them by the dozen as they just disappear.

● Go a step further and think about buying your kids' clothes in the same range of colours. Most of my children's clothes were in plain pastel colours. While it's true they might have shown the dirt more, the similar tones meant I could throw them all in the wash together without sorting and every outfit coordinated. I guarantee the one outfit that you buy with the luminous orange stripes will never get worn anyway because it will sink to the bottom of the washing basket. It will then languish there for months because there are no like colours to wash it with.

● The same principle applies to girls' tights. Only buy plain coloured ones, or you will be driven mad when the only pair you can find to go with your daughter's spotty dress are tartan. Play it safe with plain colours.

● Denim is every mother's best friend. It's easy to clean and tough, and it goes with anything. The textured colour will hide a host of sins.

● Buy clothes loose and comfy. If your child is between sizes, buy the bigger one. The looser they are, the easier it will be to dress your child – and for your child to dress himself.

● Only let your children choose their outfits within reason. Kids develop their own tastes early. However, it's not a good idea to totally give in to every little whim, or you will find yourself struggling to talk them out of a fancy dress every morning. Instead, give them a limited choice by offering two outfits they can choose from. Don't get into bad habits. If your toddler refuses to wear his winter coat on a cold morning, don't set a precedent by agreeing – just this one time – for the sake of an easy life. You are setting yourself up for endless arguments. Remember he's not in charge – you are.

● Invest in some soft thermal vests. It will save you worrying so much about whether they're keeping their coats buttoned up and scarves on.

● Bear in mind texture when you buy. Anything that's remotely scratchy on the skin will instantly be hated – and never worn.

● Cut down on those 'challenging' shopping trips. Swap kids' clothes with your friends to save on shopping time and money. Combine a coffee morning or play date with a swap shop.

● Wading through a wardrobe full of clothes that no longer fit your child wastes a lot of time, so take outgrown clothes out of circulation immediately. Keep a container for items you need to give away and another for items that need to be passed down to siblings.

● Store out-of-season clothes that your kids don't need to get to, so their current wardrobe is pared down to the essentials.

A Word About Shoes...

● Don't bother with shoes for babies who aren't
walking yet. OK, they look sweet. But they're
also completely useless and inevitably fall off.
Opt instead for good-quality baby socks that
are also designed to stay on comfortably. In my
experience and that of almost every other mum I
know, GAP baby socks usually do the trick.

● Buy a shoe measurer or download a child's foot
chart off the internet to take the guesswork out
of whether kids have outgrown their footwear.
Otherwise their cupboard will quickly descend
into a maelstrom of mismatched shoes – and
there will be arguments when your three-year-old
insists she can still wear the velvet party shoes
she wore on her second birthday. When kids' feet
are growing fast, open-toe sandals buy you a bit
more time before they need new shoes.

● For girls, patent shoes don't scuff, stay shinier
and seem to wear better.

● Don't waste time tracking down shoe polish that
exactly matches the colour of your children's
shoes and creates a crumbly mess whenever you
use it. Instead, polish them with vegetable oil to
get rid of scuffs.

● Every mum has wasted vital moments putting
shoes on the wrong foot. Draw two smiley faces
on the sides of your child's trainers so that when
the shoes are on the correct feet, the faces will
be 'looking' at each other.

● Most children can't tie their own shoes until at
least the age of seven. So until then, only buy
slip-ons or shoes with Velcro fasteners. Your

child's carers and teachers will also thank you for it because they don't have time to do up your child's shoelaces either. If you do lace, then wrap them round the ankle and double tie them at the back so there's less chance of the strings being pulled loose.

An Even Quicker Word on Heading Off Toilet Accidents...

- Always run your finger round the leg openings of a baby's nappy to make sure the frill is on the outside – or the pooh could leak out. Make sure a boy's penis is pointing down to avoid leaks. You might also want to use some toilet tissue to cover the penis when changing a boy's nappy to prevent spray.

Potty training expert Simone Cave, author of *Potty Training Boys*, also recommends these tricks:

- When you're toilet training, buy pants in bigger sizes, so they are easier for little ones to yank down in a hurry, or leave the bottom half off completely in the early stages when you're at home.

- Don't dress children in dungarees when they are learning to use the loo. They are too fiddly to get on and off. Put boys in trousers with elasticated waists and girls in easy-to-manoeuvre skirts.

- Boys can make an appalling mess while they are trying to perfect their aim. Let them use a footstool to give them a fighting chance. Make getting their aim right a game by putting a piece of loo paper in the bowl for target practice. Tell boys they will know they are aiming well if they make a loud weeing noise like daddy.

● Have flushable wipes ready by the toilet for instant wipe-ups and wiping round potties.

The Busy Mum's Guide to Teaching Your Child How to Dress Himself

Dressing kids in the morning can be one of the most stressful moments of the day. The chaos can easily descend into tears and tantrums as the clock ticks by. But remember that by the time children are three, they should be starting to help dress themselves in the mornings. Put them on the right road by showing them how to do it step by step.

First, ask them to put on their underwear. Help them stick their legs into the holes, but let them pull their pants up by themselves. Next, put their top over their head, and then let them take over. Don't practise when you are in a rush. Your child is much more likely to become flustered. Instead, have a go when you have a bit more time to spare, like at the weekend – and make it fun.

More Tips for Helping Kids to Help Themselves

● Spread out tops facedown on the bed so kids will put them on the right way.

● Tell little ones to sit down when putting on pants, trousers and socks so they don't topple over.

● Encourage youngsters to stick their heads in tops first, then put their arms through.

● Tell girls to gather up tights around their ankles first, before pulling them up their legs.

● Remind children – and particularly boys doing up trousers – to pull up zips away from their skin so they don't catch.

Keeping Ironing and Laundry to an Absolute Minimum

Keeping kids looking clean and smart can be a real challenge when you are a mum-in-a-rush. Every parent wants to take some pride in the way their child looks, even though youngsters usually have other ideas. But just a little forethought when you buy your children's clothes will save you an enormous amount of time and fuss down the line.

How to Cut Down Your Laundry Mountain

● Buy washer-and-dryer-safe mesh bags for each kid's room – one for lights and one for darks. Throw the bags directly into the washing machine and dryer – and the clothes will come out ready-sorted. If your children are old enough, give them back their laundry bags, and let them put their garments away themselves.

● If you have younger kids, go one step further when you undress them for the bath, and have a washer-safe bag ready just for socks. Throw the bag in the machine, and then all you'll need to do is pair them up and put them away.

● Have a set of play clothes – outfits for kids to wear when they are just at home getting mucky or playing, like some sweat pants and a loose sweatshirt – that don't need washing every time. The children will be able to relax and so will you.

● From around the age of two, teach your children not to wipe their noses or their mouths on their sleeves. Instead, get them into good habits by giving them a piece of paper towel at every meal so they don't wipe mucky hands and faces on clothes.

● If your kids love chocolate, try to steer them towards white chocolate rather than milk chocolate. The stains and the mess and finger smears will be considerably less serious with white chocolate buttons than with the darker versions!

● For teething or dribbly babies, head off the need to change saliva-drenched tops every few hours by buying special quick-dry dribble bibs. Less obtrusive and more comfy, you can buy them in neckerchief styles to complement your child's outfit. There's a good selection on www.babykind.co.uk.

● Do more spot cleaning. Just because your child's school sweatshirt has been worn once, it doesn't necessarily need washing right away. As long as it's stain free and the cuffs and neckline aren't too grimy, let it be worn a second time.

● Ban kids from throwing their clothes on the floor, even from a young age. Apart from making a mess, it makes you feel that you've automatically got to wash them. At first, little ones will enjoy the grown-up responsibility. Of course, it will wear off with older kids, so warn them that anything dumped on the ground will be confiscated.

● More and more primary schools are asking kids to wear school sweatshirts. While it's essential to pare a wardrobe down to the basics, this is one area where you need plenty of spares so you're not constantly laundering the only two you own. Accept hand-me-downs with open arms so you always have extras.

The Small Matter of Name Tags

When kids get to school age, attaching name tags becomes a never-ending job. But they are worth the effort for the amount of time they save you tracking down lost clothes. Here are some of the speediest methods.

● Forget sewing. Buy an indelible laundry pen so you can quickly mark your kids' property instantly. Put your phone number on the insides of coats and hats so anyone who finds them can contact you. For speed, just write your surname – unless it's very common.

● If you want to sew on name tags, don't stitch all around the edges. Instead, just loop the name tag round and put several secure stitches at one end.

● Even quicker, buy the clip-on tags, now available on the internet. Simply cut the label, fold it and fix it in place with its special clip. They won't irritate the skin and can be washed at high temperatures. Try www.nametag-it.co.uk.

● Keep iron-on tags next to your ironing pile and affix them as you work through it – though be warned that they do have a reputation for falling off after repeated washes. Also keep them for items that don't need laundering so much, like coats, scarves or bags.

How to Get Through Your Laundry Faster

When you have two jobs – as a working parent as well as a mother, you really don't want to be a laundry woman as well. Every mother knows the panic when she realizes the one item of clothing her child needs that morning is buried so deep at the bottom of the laundry pile it would take an industrial digger to get it out – or the depressing sight of an insurmountable ironing pile in the corner. But there **are** ways of keeping washing and ironing to a minimum:

● Cut the time you spend dropping off and picking up from the dry-cleaners by purchasing a dry-cleaning kit for your tumble dryer. Use it for items you shouldn't wash in water – but which also don't need pressing – like delicate jumpers and blankets.

● Never buy kids' clothing just based on whether your child will look cute in it. First have a good think about how easily the clothes will be to look after. Try crunching a section of the material and seeing what happens. If it creases easily then put it back, simple as that. Never even touch fabrics like linen. Instead, look for stretchy materials like velvetine, thicker cottons, and elastin and rayon mixes that will be wearable straight out of the washing machine.

● If you see a dry-cleaning label on an item of kids' clothing, replace it – quickly. It will get dirty on the first wearing, and by the time you get around to taking it to the cleaners, your child will probably have outgrown it anyway.

● When choosing a new machine, look for models with an optional quick-wash cycle setting for emergencies. Otherwise you could be waiting up to two hours to get one wash done.

● Get older kids into the habit of checking there are no tissues left in their shirt or trouser pockets before they put them in the laundry basket, or you'll be picking scraps off the whole washing load.

● Keep everything you need near the washing machine, on a shelf preferably at eye level. If you don't have room, try a rolling caddy that slides between the washer and dryer.

● Arrange products from left to right in the order you use them. For example, start with stain remover, then follow with bleach and detergent, then fabric softener.

● If you have several kids of the same age and sex, sorting clean laundry can be a time-consuming exercise, especially when repeated washings fade age labels. Tights are the worst – and it's often not until my seven-year-old finds she can only pull them halfway up her leg that I realize I have given her the ones meant for her three-year-old sister. Take the guesswork out. For a lightning quick way to tell clothes apart, mark the labels of each child's clothes with a different coloured nail varnish.

● In terms of making a mess, washing power is the worst, especially as it seems to get everywhere and gunks up your dispenser drawer. Instead, use powder tablets or, best of all, gel tablets that will go straight into the drum. Also worth a try are washing machine balls, which promise to clean clothes without detergent by increasing the pH of the water. They should be mess free.

● To speed things up, also buy dryer balls, which dry clothes 25 per cent quicker and reduce creases. Easy-iron fabric conditioners will also make clothes softer, more manageable and easier to press.

How to Dry Clothes So You Don't Have to Iron

● If you can, take clothes out of the machine as soon as the washing or tumble drying has finished. If they are set solid, put them back in the washing machine with a wet item to make them flexible again.

● Hang clothes like shirts immediately for the wrinkles to drop out. Fold the rest flat and smooth as soon as the cycle ends, while the clothes are still warm. The warmth will help you to smooth out the wrinkles.

● Get the biggest drying rack you have room for, ideally one that folds away. Nothing is more annoying than trying to make space for wet laundry. If you have room, hang a laundry rod from the ceiling near your washing machine or, at the very least, put up some hooks so you can hang up shirts on hangers right out of the machine. To speed the drying process during the winter, hang wet clothes on drying racks that attach to the radiator.

● Hang with the heaviest part of the garment downwards. That way many of the wrinkles will just drop out. Also use the pegs to stretch out the item so it dries wrinkle free.

● Strangely, although many of us have a setting on our machines called 'Easy Iron', few of us use it. It works by injecting a flow of cool air through the clothes towards the end of the cycle, reducing the likelihood of wrinkles.

● Don't jam the clothes into your washing machine. The more the clothes are squashed, the more creased they will come out. Keep heavy items separate, too, like towels – or they will press onto the lighter ones and wrinkle them.

● If you hang your washing on the line correctly, you won't need to iron. Hang laundry as stretched out as possible, and try not to fold it over the washing line. Use three pegs for the sides and middle and hang up each item separately without overlapping it with the next.

How to Rush Through the Ironing You Have Left

● Avoid buying clothes for you and the kids with too many buttons. They'll just slow your ironing down.

● Before you start ironing, divide your ironing piles according to their ironing temperatures. Iron the coolest temperature clothes first while the iron's heating up.

● Put a layer of tin foil underneath your ironing board cover. It will reflect heat and speed up the process.

● Don't iron things that don't need to be ironed. That includes socks, underwear and towels. Forget ironing napkins when you have dinner parties. Invest in a roll of disposable linen napkins that you can just tear off and that look as clean and ironed as the most perfect serviettes. Or, instead of doing the sheets, only do the pillowcases to make your bed look better.

● Think about buying ironing water. It will stop your iron fuzzing up and makes your clothes smell lovely. It also contains moisturizers to make textiles easier to press.

● Iron shirt seams on the wrong side first. If you are pushed for time, only do the collars.

● When the ironing is really piling high, think about whether it would be easier just to pay the local launderette. If each shirt is taking you a quarter of an hour, it's worth the money to save you time.

The School Run

Without a doubt, when kids get to school age, many mums' least favourite part of the day is the morning school run. This is a challenge that truly defines the word 'multitasking'. As well as getting yourself washed, dressed and looking presentable, the children also have to be fed, watered, groomed and teamed up with homework and sports kits. But there *are* ways to get manic mornings under control.

● Lay out everyone's clothes the night before – including your own – so you aren't rooting around for your only decent pair of tights, while chaos is gradually unfolding all around you.

● Teach kids how to pull down their cuffs when they are putting on coats so their sleeves don't get uncomfortably scrunched up.

- Yes, of course the school run would be a breeze if we all just jumped out of bed the moment the alarm went off at 5.30 a.m. But crying babies and long work hours mean it's not always possible. If you are not a natural early bird and have trouble getting out of bed in the morning, go to bed in extra warm pyjamas or nightdress and time your heating to come on early so dragging yourself out from under the duvet is not quite so painful.

- Never hit the snooze button, thinking you have time for 'five minutes more'. On school run mornings, there is an unwritten rule that says that will virtually never happen.

- If you can, get yourself dressed before getting the kids up. If you're telling them off for being in their pyjamas when you're still dripping wet and trying to keep your towel round you, the situation will rapidly deteriorate.

- Coax reluctant children out of bed on cold mornings by laying out their school clothes on the radiator to warm them up.

- Use music. One mum I know has a system which pipes music to every room in the house – and wakes her three children up simultaneously with a blast of Abba.

- If kids are tired and won't get out of bed, move their bedtime back by an hour. Experts recommend kids up to age twelve get between ten and twelve hours of sleep. Also check that older kids aren't burning the midnight oil on their computers.

- Agreeing at bedtime what kids are wearing the next day is especially important if they don't wear a uniform. Check the weather forecast the night before, and tell them any decision made the previous evening is final.

● If your kids are old enough to tell the time, try turning the clocks forward ten minutes. The children will get a move on, but you won't be rushing around like a madwoman.

● Get your kids to do the same things in the same order every morning, like getting dressed, combing hair and brushing teeth. They will soon learn automatically what they need to do next – and save you the nagging.

● Draw up a morning to-do list so they can mentally cross off each job without being reminded – as well as a list of what they need to take to school that day. Write it on a kitchen blackboard so they consider what they need to do that day over breakfast.

● Make sure toothbrushes and toothpaste are in reach for younger kids. Help little ones to stand at the sink and wash themselves by buying an anti-slip bathroom stool. Check water temperature is set so the water never gets too hot to hurt them.

● Invest in a full-length mirror. Instead of fidgeting while you try to dress them and brush their hair, you will find your children are more likely to stand still and watch their reflection.

● If they are over the age of six, put out breakfast things like cereal so kids can help themselves, even if you're not ready to make it to the kitchen. Put out bowls, spoons and cups – and anything else that doesn't need refrigeration – and let them get a head start.

- Have easy over-the-head aprons handy for those school mornings when you are serving porridge or other messy foods. If you are doing eggs, make sure they are hard boiled so there is less risk of getting runny egg yolk on their school clothes.

- Make hurrying up a game for the younger ones. To speed your child along when necessary, set a timer and say: 'Let's try to get dressed before the buzzer goes off.'

- Ban younger kids from taking toys to school. You will find they focus on the toy rather than leaving the house. When it gets forgotten at the end of the day – or, worse still, lost – you will have a drama on your hands.

- While the weather is mild, remember that short socks are much quicker to put on than knee-length ones.

- Have everything you need at hand by the door, like book bags, gym kits and library books. It's so easy to forget things when you're in a hurry.

- Put up a hook somewhere convenient and get into the habit of automatically putting your keys there to avoid panicky searches for the car keys when it's time to leave. That way, they also won't get left on sideboards and covered over with mail, papers or other debris.

- For girls, cut down the time you spend zipping and buttoning their coats by buying ponchos, preferably with a hood, that they can throw on over anything in an instant and still stay warm.

- Threading gloves on strings through your kids' coats usually just leads to tangles. Get some Mitt

Clips – double-ended pieces of elastic with clips – to keep kids' gloves attached to their sleeves and ready to put on. You can buy them online at www.snugasabug.com. Old suspender clips will also work.

● Thread scarves through coat loops, so they are ready to wrap round your child's neck as soon as he puts on his coat.

● If you drive to school, stock up your car's glove compartment with cereal bars, oatcakes or dried fruit for late mornings, so at least kids can top up on breakfast if you're behind. Also keep a supply of wipes handy to wipe up any messy faces or food stains left over from breakfast.

● Think of yourself, too. If you've been up for an hour and a half and still haven't had a morsel to eat, your blood sugar will be dropping fast – and you're bound to be snappy. For hectic mornings, have oatcakes and drinking yoghurts on hand for you too, so you can stay even tempered.

● If you walk to school or nursery, speed it up by getting your child a scooter. It means instead of her dragging along behind you, you will find that finally you are struggling to keep up!

How to Fix Kids' Hair Faster...

If you have daughters, you will know how much screaming and shouting can accompany even the most harmless attempt to get your girls groomed. Try these short cuts to get through it without the trauma.

● Get the softest bristle brush you can so your

daughters aren't afraid of getting scratched on the face with bristles.

● Avoid novelty accessories. Anything with too much ornamentation can easily get tangled up in girls' hair. Don't use any accessories that are too heavy, either. They will slip and dangle, and pull out delicate hair with them.

● Even if your little girl insists on long hair, don't let it grow any longer than shoulder length – and certainly not down to the elbow.

● Keep a pair of hair-cutting scissors in the house – to trim every few weeks. That way you should only need to go to the hairdresser every three months for a 'shape'. Play hair salons to make it more fun, but make it clear it's a game they should only play with grown-ups. I say this after my four-year-old walked into my office with her shoulder-length mane hacked into a pudding bowl.

● Tell kids you are taking them for a 'trim' not a 'cut', or they will get frightened of what it will entail.

● Never buy hair bands with metal bits; they break the hair. Instead, buy thick comfy towelling ones so you won't spend painful minutes disentangling them.

● Don't fix your child's hair in the same way every day. It creates kinks and weak spots.

● Let kids' hair dry naturally as much as possible. But don't send them to bed with wet hair, as it will rough up the hair shaft and make it tangled.

● Head off discoloured, dull 'swimming pool hair' by getting children to rinse beforehand in plain water. The coating of water will stop the pool

79

chemicals from penetrating the hair shaft. Then rinse again as soon as they get out to prevent damage. Making your child wear a swimming cap will also protect their locks.

- To make it easier the next morning, give girls their own mini brush and encourage them to brush out their hair every night at bedtime. Put their hair in loose braids to keep it neat and knot free for the following day.

- If you find a bad knot, pull it apart with your fingers first. Then spray it with spray-on conditioner. Use a wide-tooth comb and hold the hair close to the root to stop it tugging and hurting.

- The starting point for a neat kids' hairstyle is a parting. First, sweep the hair from side to side to see where the parting falls naturally. Then, develop the rough line with the thin end of a comb or a pencil. Don't make the mistake I made and assume that all partings lie naturally in the middle. You will just be fighting a losing battle. If the hair naturally falls to the side, don't fight it!

- Anyone who has girls has hair bows and hair accessories scattered everywhere. Get to the right ones faster by putting them in a see-through plastic organizer on the back of her bedroom door. Buy in the same colours so they always coordinate.

Chapter 4

Not Now, Mum...

How to head off tantrums before they happen and get kids to do what you ask the first time – not the twentieth

When you're a mum with loads on your plate, you want the time with your kids to be rewarding and enjoyable – not a marathon of nagging, whingeing and bartering. Do you dare to imagine how much valuable time you would save as a parent if your children did what you asked, when you asked them to do it?

It may seem ridiculously simple to say it, but it really does boil down to just two principles: consistency and boundaries, served up with a lot of love and praise. Of course, like everything in parenting, it's easier in principle than in practice. But it will definitely spare you and your kids endless rows and tantrums if you sit down and consciously decide what those boundaries are – and lay them out for everyone to agree, respect and remember. If you stick to the basics and make sure the kids also know what they are, you might even get them to listen the first time – instead of the fifteenth.

The Seven Most Likely Sins of Harassed Parents

1. Shouting to Get Kids to Do Things

TIME-WASTING: Yelling at the top of your voice may work the first time by shocking your kids into submission. But the novelty quickly wears off, and you'll simply teach them to scream back at you. Shouting at kids from another room to chivvy them into brushing their teeth or getting dressed is also a waste of time. You are simply giving them the chance to say they can't hear you. Pretty quickly, it escalates into a nerve-jangling shouting fest.

TIME-SAVING: As far as is realistically possible, stop what you are doing for a moment, go into the room where they are, make eye contact, and tell them what you want in a low, clear, authoritative voice that makes it clear what you expect them to do. If necessary, get down on their level, so they know you mean business. Believe me, just a little eye contact goes a very long way!

2. Not Being Clear About the Rules

TIME-WASTING: If you make up rules on an ad hoc, as-and-when basis, you will confuse your kids. You will also be inviting time-consuming conflict, because your children will think they have got room for manoeuvre and will try to argue the point. If you are feeling a bit tired and fuzzy, you may also forget exactly what you said before, leaving your kids to push the boundaries even further to see where they lie.

TIME-SAVING: Head off conflict by setting out your house rules in advance and sticking to them. Let older children have some input so it all feels more democratic, and tell them adults will be abiding by them too. Make them realistic for the ages of your children. Then write the list on a large, colourful piece of paper and stick it where the whole family can see it.

Writing the rules down in black and white also means you and your partner will be on the same page, as well as caregivers coming into your home, like grandparents and babysitters. You, too, will probably want to refer to the list when your own resolve is feeling a bit shaky. When you're tired, when you've had a long day, they are always there – like the Ten Commandments. It works almost instantly because the rules become the bottom line which your children know they can't argue with.

Sample List of House Rules

Each family is different, and the rules may need to be re-drawn slightly as new challenges arise. But this is a starter list for a family with kids from toddler age to about eight. Make the rules as simple and clear as possible. Ask the children to suggest them and work out themselves – with your help – why they are important.

Start off with no more than eight and make them positive, not negative, instructions. Underline the fact that they apply to everyone in the home – even the grown-ups – so they feel fair. Finally, make them realistic and achievable for your children's ages. Give plenty of praise when they stick to them.

a. We are gentle. We do not hurt, push or hit each other.

b. We are kind. We treat others as we would like to be treated.

c. We do our homework without making excuses.

d. We use our nice voices – or we do not get heard.

e. We respect the fact that sometimes we have to wait patiently.

f. We help put our toys away and keep our rooms tidy.

g. We tell the truth.

h. We remember that this family is a team who help each other to be happy and have a home that we all enjoy.

3. Negotiating Too Much

TIME-WASTING: Although many parents believe they are being sensitive by letting kids have an opinion on everything from what to eat to what to wear, nothing could be further from the truth. It's a habit especially hard to break for working parents who feel guilty for not being around – and think they are respecting their children's individuality. But it may surprise you that deep down kids actually want to be told what to do – and are frightened when they feel in control. No child wants a total lack of structure.

TIME-SAVING: You can, however, give them a restricted selection of choices. For example: 'You can stay inside and watch *Art Attack* or go outside and play football. Which of these two things do you want to do?' Don't give the child carte blanche, but let them choose between two equally good options. They don't have to know you are happy whichever one they choose.

4. Entering into a Debate

TIME-WASTING: Even when they've made a decision, many parents make the mistake of trying to reason and explain it. Kids will seize on it as a golden opportunity to try to wear you down. The other common mistake is to make requests sound optional. If you want your child to have a bath, but it comes out sounding like a question, then your child will inevitably take advantage by saying no, and you will have a row on your hands.

TIME-SAVING: Don't enter into a debate. Don't ask; tell. Once you have made your decision, keep any explanation brief. If absolutely necessary, make direct eye contact and state clearly in thirty words or less why that's the rule. Don't feel guilty about asserting yourself. As a parent, that's your job.

5. Giving In

TIME-WASTING: Time pressures can mean that in the limited amount of time you have with your kids, you want to make it all perfect. Furthermore, parents can fall into the trap of thinking that saying yes to their children all the time makes their kids happy. The problem gets worse, say experts, when parents who were brought up in a very disciplinarian way during their own childhood decide to behave the opposite way with their own kids. But give in and the kids will keep pressing your buttons on the off-chance they'll hit the jackpot.

TIME-SAVING: Set limits and stick to them. It makes kids feel safer. Otherwise they will feel insecure and will push you to see what you are going to do about it. Remember that as a parent, if you don't say no, you are not doing your job properly.

6. Feeling Guilty

TIME-WASTING: So many parents start off laying down the law, and then ruin it by worrying they have been unfair when the child cries and screams. Because as adults we know we would have to be seriously upset to become so hysterical, we fear we must have gone over the top when kids shed tears. The fact is that most children can weep at the drop of a hat; that's the way they are wired. Many's the time when I have been amazed by seeing my kids go from a zero to sixty tantrum – and just as rapidly back to zero again.

TIME-SAVING: Stick to your guns. Unless you are stressed or have completely got the wrong end of the stick, your initial instincts were probably right. Pretend you are somewhere else if you have to be or go into autopilot to hold your line. Make it clear that when Mummy says no, she really means no. If necessary, repeat it like a mantra until they get the message. Otherwise, clear your diary for an endless round of exhausting tantrums and whinge-fests – and I mean exhausting for you, not them.

7. Feeding Kids Snack Foods

TIME-WASTING: When many mums hear the words 'I'm hungry', they feel duty bound to swing into action. For the sake of a quiet life, you may also have fallen into the trap of feeding them a constant stream of snack foods like crisps or biscuits. But although they may be happy for a moment, it's not long before the sugar content sends their insulin levels on a roller coaster, creating hyperactivity – followed by more hunger pangs. Before you know it, they are back again wanting more.

TIME-SAVING: Give kids slow-release protein snacks like cheese strings, nuts and pumpkin seeds. They can be just as fun. Their blood sugar levels will even out; they will calm down; and they'll be fuller for longer.

How to Put a Stop to Whining

Whining not only shatters the nerves of every hassled parent; it also eats up an amazing amount of time. Make no mistake: that constant drip, drip, drip is meant to grind you down – until you can't bear it a second longer. So before you or your child wastes another moment, here are some tactics to head it off before it starts.

- Never cave in. It's not easy to deal with, especially when you're tired, overworked and are just praying for peace and quiet. Even if you've done valiantly by holding out nine times, don't think it's OK to submit on the tenth – or your child will think he's learnt how to break you and will keep trying for longer.

- Ask children not to use 'the whiny voice', and tell them it's because you can't understand them. Draw attention to how it sounds by talking back to them in the same tone. Instruct them to use their normal, nice voice instead. When they do request something nicely, look at them, smile and say thank you.

- Nip whingeing in the bud by acknowledging what kids are asking for the first time they say it. Make sure they know you have heard them by looking at them, repeating what they have just said back to them and giving the appropriate response. Even if it's not the answer they want, at least they know you've taken it on board.

- Always deliver on a promise. If you say you are coming to play with them, honour it. Don't kid yourself you can squeeze in five minutes of housework first without them noticing, however worthy your aim, otherwise they won't trust you to do what you say and will become even more needy.

● Check what TV programmes they are watching. You might be surprised by the undesirable behaviour of some of the characters. Programme-makers may well argue that there's a moral at the end of the show, but your child is more likely to take away the bratty behaviour than the life lesson.

● If you are taking your child to a place where it's especially important that they behave, set some ground rules before you leave. Tell them they will only be rewarded at a very clearly defined end-time – and only if they have earned it. Don't make the reward something you have to buy when you are out, otherwise the whole trip will turn into a nag-marathon about how soon they can have it. Instead, promise a game or trip to the park.

● When dealing with older kids who whine, ask them to pay ten pence out of their pocket money into a glass jar for charity each time they succumb. That way they can see how much they are doing it and will feel the consequences.

● Watch your own whining. Are you constantly moaning to your partner, tutting, sighing, huffing and raising your eyes to high heaven? Be honest and double check your children are not learning bad habits from you. Try to go a day without complaining to start with, and then keep going.

● Make sure your kids are getting enough sleep and getting a proper diet that's keeping their blood sugar at an even level. Sometimes they might just be tired and hungry.

● If older kids have a more general complaint – like they are not allowed the same privileges as their friends – ask them to write it all down so you can really hear what they are saying without it descending into a row. It will get it out of their system, and once it's down in black and white, it may not seem so important to them after all. They will also feel you are taking their grievance seriously.

● Use some humour to break the mood. Join in and mimic a silly voice to call attention to how ridiculous it sounds – and tell *them* how you want a million pounds, a new car, a designer wardrobe and all the rest. Children need to learn they won't get everything they want in life.

The Busy Mum's Sixty-Second Discipline Plan: How to Deal with Tricky Situations in One Minute Flat

When really bad behaviour strikes, it's vital to act fast so the incident doesn't turn into a protracted row. Not only will you save time, you will save your nerves as well.

Nought to five seconds

Take away the problem: Whether your son has had a popcorn fight with his best mate in his bedroom or your toddler has bitten her big sister, step in right away. If necessary, move your child away from the scene of the drama or put the warring parties in different rooms to instantly defuse the situation.

Five to Fifteen seconds

Breathe deeply: No one will blame you for being angry if your children have done something awful. But try to fill your lungs first so you don't do or say something you'll be sorry for. Some parents think yelling is a way of telling their kids how serious the offence is. In fact, you are wasting your time because all your child will see is you acting like a hysterical maniac – and that conveniently takes their minds off what they've done wrong. If you want your child to get the message, stay in control.

Fifteen to Thirty seconds

Find out what happened: Has your four-year-old hacked off her sister's hair because she's just seen you at the hairdresser's? Is your son climbing on the kitchen counter because he wants to be Spiderman? It won't excuse the situation, but understanding it may help you deal with it better. Don't waste time repeatedly asking rhetorical 'whys?'. Children won't know how to answer.

Forty-five to Sixty seconds

Talk to your child: Get down to the child's level, and look him in the eye. Tell him what's he's done wrong and what he should have done differently, preferably using just two or three sentences. Then let the issue drop. Don't dish out the punishment automatically. Simply removing the child from the situation and ending the game may be enough for him to understand the consequences of what he's done. Only crack down harder if it was premeditated and you've repeatedly told the child not to do it before.

Other Time-Consuming Hassles You Don't Need...

Lending and borrowing toys: 'Neither a borrower nor a lender be' doesn't just apply to money. It applies to toys too. By all means get kids into good habits by letting them share on play dates, but discourage them taking others' toys from the house. If another child offers to let them take one home, just politely decline and say your child will look forward to coming to play with the item next time. Having the responsibility of looking after another child's property will eventually boil down to you – and returning it in one piece is one more thing you don't need on your overloaded to-do list. With older children, a lending and borrowing ban also saves all sorts of misunderstandings.

Swapping toys with siblings: This can also apply to siblings. In my house, there used to be endless bartering and promises about what the other child could keep for ever and ever, followed by rows over who really owned what. Sharing is fine, but when toys get given away, everyone loses track and the rows begin again. Save the giving for birthdays and Christmas.

Children repeating themselves: If you work from home and have children over the age of eight, ask them to limit the number of times they yell for attention. If you do not answer them after the second time they've yelled 'Mum!', they should assume you are busy and will come to see what they want as soon as you are finished. If they're still not sure, tell them that the fact your office door is closed means you can't be disturbed unless it's an emergency or someone's at the door. But you also have to stick to your part of the bargain, by seeing to what they want as soon as you are free.

Making yourself a doormat: To begin with, whenever my three-year-old dropped something, she would demand I pick it up – although she was quite capable of doing it herself. It quickly became clear she regarded treating Mummy like a slave as entertaining, until I made it a general house rule that whoever drops an object, retrieves it. Remember that kids would have you waiting on them hand and foot for ever if they could get away with it. So don't make more work for yourself by being a walk-over.

How to Stop Sibling Rivalry

Sibling rivalry is not all bad; it teaches kids how to negotiate, share and stand up for themselves. But when you're a hassled mum, there are times when listening to kids bickering over toys, calling each other names or hitting each other is the most exhausting part of being a parent. If your head's already overloaded, the added stress of hearing 'Mummy, he hit me' for the tenth time can, frankly, be the final straw. Of course, there is a whole library of books on the subject – but, as you don't have the time to read them, this is basically what you need to know.

Talk to them: A large part of sibling rows is indignation. So take each child aside at a quiet time and ask them for their point of view. Make them see that you understand how they feel when their brothers and sisters annoy them. Tell them what it was like for you growing up with your siblings, if it helps. At the same time, also explain how the other child feels when they ignore, shout at or snatch from them.

Ask them to sort it out: With older kids, you can also ask them to negotiate the solution themselves. Listen to both sides equally, acknowledge what both have to say, and tell them you have confidence that they will work it out. Come back later and find out how they did it – and if it was successful, explain exactly what they did right.

Don't dodge the issue: Get to the point and ask them precisely what they don't like about their siblings. It might yield an explanation you'd previously never dreamt of. For a time, my daughter Lily, then six, was behaving so badly around her younger sister that life was becoming intolerable. When asked why, she explained she hated the fact that Clio could be at home with me after morning nursery was finished, while she had to stay at school till four. Then she floored me by saying that she was even more angry because she would soon be sent away to boarding school. I was able to reassure her that we'd never contemplated any such thing, and that she could be at home with us for as long as she wanted. Her anxiety subsided, and her behaviour towards her sister improved overnight. But if I hadn't asked her, I wouldn't have had a clue. So really try to find out what the resentments are that are building up in your child's head. You could be surprised.

Set boundaries: Sit down with your kids and discuss how they would like to be treated by a sibling and how they should behave back. But make sure they know the bottom line – and that it is never acceptable to snatch, bite or push. Watch for sneaky, covert hitting or shoving when your back is turned. Tell them that it's fine to vent anger, but not through violence. Help find them another outlet, like kicking a football or pummelling a cushion.

Give praise: When they are sharing well or just enjoying an activity together, describe precisely why you're pleased with their behaviour. Say things like:

'I love the way you helped each other to make a new house for your action figures.'

Label them positively: Make them believe they are good sharers or kind siblings by telling them that's what they are.

Give special time: Ask yourself honestly if you are really paying your kids enough attention when you are with them. After all, fighting with a sibling is a guaranteed way to get Mummy off the phone or the computer. Give each child defined 'mummy time', and make it clear that it's a period you want to spend just with them. This could mean nothing more than an errand to the shops, a walk in the park together or a board game. It can be miraculous how quickly this transforms a sulky, bolshy youngster into an angel, because he feels secure that you not only love him, but you also want to spend time with him.

Don't take sides: Treat each child equally. It sounds obvious, but it's easy to favour the younger, cuter child, compared to a bad-tempered elder sibling. If you find you are losing patience with one child and starting to prefer another, spend more time with the difficult one to try to reconnect.

Never compare: Make each child feel special in a different way and help them develop different talents. Sensitive kids are often looking to keep score and spot slights against them, so make sure you show the same positive body language and facial expressions to each.

Encourage teamwork: Let them play on a team against you and your partner, or encourage them to form a band. Show them how they can help each other. When one child hurts himself, ask his sibling to look after him. Ask the older child to help the younger one do something he can't do. When I asked my elder daughter, Lily, to design her sister's nativity play costume, they spent hours happily trying out different angel outfits – and Lily's general irritation with her sister was turned into pride. Foster some team spirit, and make sure that everyone in your household feels they are on the same side.

And One Other Helpful Hint to Improve Behaviour...

Tell your kids you like them: For my money, just telling your children you like them works wonders for their behaviour and self-esteem. Of course, they expect you to love them – you're their parent. You probably tell them a dozen times a day, and they take it for granted. But choose a moment now and again to tell them you *like* them too. It's something totally different. It means you think they have grown into worthwhile, nice people whom you respect and want to spend time with. At the appropriate moment, take each aside and tell them. I guarantee their faces will light up.

How to Get Kids to Do Their Homework

For many parents, cajoling and pleading with kids to do their homework is a nightly battle they could really do without at the end of a hard day. Evenings should be precious times when parents can reconnect with kids – not a time-consuming battle of wills. Here's how to get kids to do their homework without a row.

Make sure kids get a break first: Most children need a rest when they get home from school. Don't forget they're often starving, and you can't expect them to study on an empty stomach. So give them a high-protein snack like a chicken drumstick, nuts or an oatcake with peanut butter to steady their blood sugar levels and help them concentrate.

Get the timing right: There are three obvious times for children to get down to homework: shortly after they get home from school, before supper and after supper. Because all kids have different energy levels, let them choose when they want to do it – and then stick to it.

Get into the habit early: You can start laying the groundwork for good habits at a young age. If your child is in nursery or reception, make sure they have some quiet time when they get home from school, either with a story or a board game. If you have older kids who need to do homework, get the younger ones to do drawing or quiet 'work' activities at the same time.

Set up a homework centre: For older kids, make a special place for study that includes a desk, sharpened pencils, rubbers and reference books. Don't assume the best place is the bedroom, because it can be hard to concentrate in the room where you play and sleep. If your child is fidgety, check that the chair is comfortable, placed squarely at the table and pushed all the way in. If you have space, buy a child-sized desk. Make your youngster proud of it by letting them decorate it with achievement stickers.

Keep them equipped: Buy them pencils with rubbers at the end, so they are not searching for an eraser to correct mistakes. Don't skimp on cheap pencil sharpeners either. The budget plastic ones just splinter pencils and leave you or your child trying to fish out the lead. Instead, invest in a substantial heavy-duty model, with a collecting barrel attached, so the shavings don't fall on the floor.

Keep it positive: Praise your youngster when they're trying hard, especially when they find it difficult. It's easy after a long day to lose your patience. Don't get angry when they make mistakes or they'll lose confidence. If they get a right answer, say 'Great'. If they make a mistake, say 'Nearly', and let them have another go.

Cut out distractions: Given the chance, children will find endless excuses not to study – so head them off before they come up. Suggest kids have their snack first and also go to the loo beforehand. Nothing is more distracting than a TV, so turn it off even if it's not in the same room. Don't let them hear you talking on the phone either.

Talk to the teacher: If your child has weekly tests to revise for, ask the teacher what learning style suits them best. Children learn in different ways. Some learn by seeing and reading, others by hearing or writing it down. There may be lots of fun ways to learn the times tables, such as making words out of play dough or turning the times tables into a song.

Check it's not too difficult: The real reason your child is putting off homework may be because it's too hard, and they are getting discouraged and anxious. Sometimes teachers fail to make enough allowances for mixed abilities in the classroom. So if a task is aimed at the average ability level, it could mean that as many as a third of the class struggle. Tell the teacher if your child is having problems.

Don't expect too much too soon: Most kids are aged seven before they can sit down and work at home independently. Before that, they will need an adult to sit down near them. Older kids may also need you to help pace them and switch from one subject to another. Experts agree that while it's a good idea to be around your child when they study, hovering over them is not. When you do need to get involved, keep it brief and encouraging with remarks such as, 'You're on the right track' or 'Keep it up'.

Don't take too much on yourself: Remember that at the end of the day, homework is your child's job, not yours. Ask yourself whether the reason you are really getting so involved is because they need it – or you are being a competitive parent. The idea of homework is to get children into good study patterns, not to do it for them. Look on your main role as bringing up your child in a household where learning is generally encouraged.

Be a role model: When your youngster is doing their homework, do yours at the same time by getting down to tasks such as sorting paperwork and paying bills. It sends a message that grown-ups have homework too.

Be reasonable: Don't expect your child to jump with glee at every piece of homework they get. As adults, it's easy to forget we are much freer to avoid things we don't like. But kids have no choice but to spend time on subjects they may not enjoy. If your child asks why they have to do homework, be sympathetic but also realistic. If they say they hate maths, explain that it's a means to an end – and they may need that qualification to study the subject they do like in the future.

A Short Word on Star Charts

Nothing quite focuses a child's mind like a star chart. Used consistently, it can be a fantastic short cut to good behaviour. But not all rewards systems are created equal. Don't let your system get too complicated, or eventually it will fizzle out. Don't make it up as you go along either. Instead, give it some thought before you introduce the idea to your children.

Decide what you are going to give stars for and how many are needed for the treat; otherwise they will try to push for more at every opportunity, and it won't feel special any more. So try focusing on the aspect of your child's behaviour you most want to change first, and use the stars to reward those successes. If it's a nightly struggle to get your child to do his homework, start off with that until you get a regular routine going. Instead of adding more toys to their collection, make the end treat an activity, like some weekend cake-baking.

Other Ways of Getting Your Kids to Do What They Need to Do Without Being Asked a Hundred Times...

Teeth Brushing

- Don't keep begging your child to clean his teeth. Tell him.

- Make it more fun by letting your youngster choose his own special toothbrush – and even his own brand of kids' toothpaste – so that he feels proud and involved.

- Make up a tooth-brushing song, or really go the whole hog and buy an electric toothbrush that plays a tune to keep him scrubbing. Or buy a toothbrush-holder egg timer to keep him brushing for at least one minute.

- Little ones don't really see the point of brushing teeth. So explain that they will be scrubbing off the yellow and getting minty fresh breath and pearly white teeth instead.

- Clean your teeth at the same time and ask them to play copycat with you.

Hair Washing and Bath Time

Almost every child goes through a phase when they scream blue murder every single time you come near them with a glob of shampoo. I have literally seen my kids turn into Linda Blair from *The Exorcist* – biting and clawing to get out of the bath – as if I were trying to murder them, not wash their hair. Still, it has to be done. So for your own sake, as well as theirs, make it as painless – and quick – as possible.

● Head off the conflict before it starts, and cut back on the number of hair washes. Until adolescence, most kids' hair doesn't get really dirty for a couple of weeks.

● Find out what the problem is by letting your child wash their doll's hair in the bath – and see what it reveals. Suggest they wash their toy's hair at the same time to give them something to focus on.

● Let them help. Maybe they just want to help control the process or help hold the showerhead.

● Obviously, the shorter the hair, the easier it is. But if you want your little girl to grow it long, keep it to the shoulder, so it's long enough for bunches and plaits, but it doesn't become unmanageable. Invest in a good bath hat, so hair doesn't trail in soapy water in the bath and become tangled and ratty-looking.

● Use a thick sponge and gently squeeze the water over their heads to get them used to the sensation. They might even find it tickles. It's less intimidating than a jug-full. As long as they've only grown a bit of hair, this will be all it takes to rinse out the shampoo.

● If you're really on borrowed time – but your child's hair is a rat's nest – try a combined shampoo/conditioner, followed by a spray detangler to cut the number of applications and rinses.

● Give them something to look at. Take their mind off the process by sticking a plastic mirror at the end of the bath and using the shampoo foam to style their hair into mad styles – like a teddy bear's ears or Shrek's ogre ears.

● Get in with them. With much younger kids, feeling you supporting them will make them feel a lot more secure. For children who feel unsafe in a big tub, buy a bath ring, which will enable them to sit up, or a bucket-shaped wash pod. It will also free your arms up to get the job done more efficiently.

● Change tactics: For older children, try using the sink to wash their hair. Get your child to tip their head back and look at the ceiling. If they've seen you at the hairdresser's, pretend they are also getting their hair done.

● Stick funny pictures on the ceiling above the bath so they have something to focus on when they tip their heads back to get their hair rinsed. Sing a special hair-washing song so they know the process won't last long.

● Draw a line across their foreheads with petroleum jelly to stop the shampoo running into their eyes.

● Get your kids swimming early so they get used to the sensation of water on their faces. Use their goggles in the bath to keep water out of their eyes.

● Use character gloves to make face-washing fun. Tell them Mr Monkey – or whoever – wants to kiss their face all over. Let the toys also help with hair-rinsing.

● Save yourself stress by making sure your bathroom taps can't get dangerously hot.

How to Get the Kids to Go to Bed without a Fuss

As much as we love our children, it's been said that we love them a little bit more when they are asleep. Here's how to get them to bed on time – for their sake and, frankly, for ours too.

Make it special time: Set aside twenty minutes to have special time with your children. Keep it calm and relaxed, but make sure they know it will not go beyond the period you have set aside to be together. Chat to them about how they are feeling to relieve any anxieties before bed.

Be consistent: Even if you have a guilt attack and decide you haven't seen enough of your kids that day, stick to your routine. Make a ritual out of putting on night clothes, brushing teeth and having a set amount of stories. Be consistent and don't give in to requests for more than the allocated amount. As you reach the end of the last book, gently prepare your child to say good night by telling them how many pages are left.

Head off requests: Have a glass of water next to the bed, their night light illuminated and their favourite toy next to them to keep them company when you're not there. Remind them that they need to ask for what they want before a set time, and tell them after that the moment is gone.

Try story tapes: It depends on your child, but some kids are happier to have lights out if they can listen to their favourite story tape or song tape quietly after you've gone.

Don't pressure them: Repeatedly telling children to go to sleep and warning they will be tired in the morning will only make them more anxious when they can't drop off. Instead, tell them to relax, and reassure them that lying quietly in bed is almost as good.

A final word: Never underestimate the power of music to help influence kids' behaviour. It works at the deepest levels. Whether it's fun, energetic music to get them out of bed and off to school, funny songs to break a bad mood, or gentle sounds to help them unwind at bedtime, it can all reinforce your message. But use it wisely, and let kids develop their own musical tastes.

Chapter 5

Are We There Yet?

How to save time and stress when you're on the road with your kids – and how to make other special occasions easier

Venturing further afield with kids – and sometimes even to the end of the road – can be a daunting prospect. As they grow, keeping kids happy, well fed and tidy when you are out and about takes the foresight of a seer and the patience of a saint. I have often marvelled at the amount of packing I have had to do to cover for every eventuality just for a weekend stay with grandparents. So here's how to make it all that much easier.

Weekends Away and Holidays

Pack a laundry bag: You won't have the nasty job of weeding the dirty clothes from the unused stuff, and you can empty it into the washing machine as soon as you get home.

Take a dressing gown: When staying away, you don't want to be pulling towels around you so you can leave your room to attend to a crying child. Take a dressing gown for an easy cover up.

Stay coordinated: Pack each of your kids' clothes in a particular range of colours. When you arrive, you'll be able to dress them more quickly because everything will go together.

Don't fold; roll: Rolling clothes up is quicker and more space efficient than folding. You can even roll complete outfits together.

Bundle outfits: Go one step further and roll together the complete outfit for each day – including pants and socks – in a freezer bag. It will save you time you would otherwise spend rummaging through the bottom of your suitcase.

How to Make Time in the Car Go Faster

While some babies drop off to sleep as soon as they hear the hum of the engine, there are just as many who scream their heads off from the second you put your key into the ignition to the minute you pull up the handbrake. And it doesn't get any easier as they get older. They just get better at asking for things.

The moment kids are buckled in for a long journey, they quickly figure out they are not the only ones who are captive – you are too. Throw boredom and frustration into the mix and the result can be an endless catalogue of demands, many of which you are powerless to do anything about while you are on the road. Few journeys will be entirely stress free. But there are ways to make

them pass more quickly – and with fewer infuriating 'Are
we there yets?'

Every Trip

● Get into the habit of putting the keys straight
into the ignition as soon as you open the car
door. After ten minutes of buckling in, pacifying
and loading up the boot, you will be surprised by
how easily those keys can go astray, drop down
the backs of seats or even fall into the gutter.

● Fit sunshades into the rear windows. Remember
that kids can't move freely in their seats, so it's
hardly surprising they are annoyed to have the
sun shining in their eyes. Try adhesive ones or the
kind that stick on with suction cups.

● Keep a stash of loose change in the car. There's
simply no such thing as just popping into a shop
for change for the machine when you've got kids in
tow. Spare yourself the stress and build up a store
of loose change – but out of sight. It only takes a
few pounds on view to tempt a thief to break in.

Longer Journeys

● Map reading is hard enough, without adding kids.
Now that the price of satellite navigation systems
is becoming more affordable, it is well worth
considering. Don't leave yourself entirely at its
mercy though. The British Society for the Prevention
of Accidents suggests that all drivers take five
minutes to look at the map before setting off to
get an overall idea of the route. It means that if
you get distracted – or your child is screaming over
the top of the instructions – you still have a good
general idea of where you're heading.

- Don't underestimate how hard it is to be confined in a back seat for long periods. Plan ahead and check for parks and playgrounds en route so kids can let off steam on the way.

- Pack water bottles with sports tops that are easy to open and close, and fit snugly into cup holders.

- Take easy snacks. Certain foods travel well when you're making long trips, like oatcakes and mini bagels. Carrot sticks, celery and peanut butter, and Marmite and cheese sandwiches also stay appetizing and don't make too much mess.

- Get older kids involved by giving them their own maps and marking the route with a pen. Ask them to help navigate and look for interesting features along the way.

- Use a shoe organizer with lots of compartments, tied to the back of the front seat in front, to store a good selection of boredom-busting toys for kids. Good ideas include a compass, binoculars, window wax crayons and stickers.

- Pack one towel in the back seat for every child. It can be used as a blanket, a mop for any spills, or on toddlers' laps to help toys stay put. You can also tuck one end into the window and hang it as a curtain to keep out the sun.

- Most toddlers won't last happily in the car for more than two hours at a stretch. So cut journey time as much as possible by using motorways.

- For longer journeys, get a car seat with a clip-on tray so kids have somewhere to rest their toys. Swap children around in their seats to stop them getting bored.

- Even if you absolutely hate the thought of

hypnotizing your kids with TV, a long journey is probably the one time when it's in *your* best interests to make an exception, so consider investing in an in-car DVD player. Remember you need a break too; constantly having to turn round to cater to every whim is a painful experience.

● Consider letting older kids have personal MP3 players, unless you want to play DJ with your car stereo and referee arguments about whose CD is due to be put on next.

What You Really Need in a Car

A roadside assistance membership card: It really, really is an emergency when you've broken down and have got young kids with you, so make sure you've got a phone number and membership number at hand. When you are ferrying kids around, you will inevitably leave the lights on at least once and will need help with a flat battery.

Spare scarves, hats and gloves: So you don't have to run back into the house at the last minute.

A brush and hair accessories: For manic mornings when you haven't had a chance to deal with your children's hair.

Umbrellas galore: Buy the broadest, toughest ones you can get. Don't bother with children's brollies until the age of about six. They don't really have the patience, control or strength to hold them up until then.

Pac-a-macs: Buy loose-fitting all-in-one styles with hoods, big enough to pull on over coats.

Sunscreen: Buy the highest SPF you can find. Make application quick and easy by only buying the aerosol versions.

A travel potty: Even bigger children will end up being grateful for it.

A first aid kit: Be prepared with a kit containing bandages, a foil blanket, dressings, tape and, crucially, plasters. Hopefully you won't need it. But nothing proves to a wailing child with a minor scrape that you are taking him seriously more than a plaster.

Wellington boots in a shoe bag: So you can leave them to dry out in the car – and stop the caked-on mud crumbling everywhere when it hardens.

A square holdall: Most children seem to view their parents as their personal porters and think it's OK to offload everything the moment they see you at the school gates. Keep a holdall for those times when you haven't got eight arms to carry musical instruments, book bags, lunch boxes and ballet outfits.

Extra nappies: Only for the first couple of years, obviously, but a secret stash in the boot will often come in useful, not least because when you are on the move, an open boot is the easiest place to discreetly change a baby. They are also handy for general mop-ups.

A satellite navigation system: Don't rely on it though. Also pack an A to Z and atlas too.

Wipes and tissues: Useful for cleaning dirty faces and bottoms – and even giving the interior of the car a quick clean when you have a spare 5 minutes.

Defroster and ice scraper: Frost can wreak havoc with your school-run timetable. Make sure you are equipped with both for winter mornings.

Kids' song and story CDs: They will keep them quiet for a while, and the upside of being trapped in the car with your children is that they are a captive audience for alphabet, number and times tables discs.

Spare pens and pencils: For scribbling down shop phone numbers and allowing kids to start their homework in the back when you're between appointments.

Lip gloss: For morale-boosting touch-ups.

Balls and skipping ropes: Keep them ready so you are always prepared for the park.

Towels: These can be used as blankets, clean-ups or car window curtains.

A plastic rubbish bag in the driver side door: As you get out of the car, put all the snotty tissues, food wrappers and the rest in it, so your car doesn't become a pigsty on wheels.

How to Make Time Go Faster on an Aeroplane

If long car journeys can be challenging, at least the dramas are played out in the relative privacy of your vehicle. Take your kids on a plane, and there will be roughly 200 tutting strangers, praying you and your family won't be sitting anywhere near them. Ignore them, of course, but for your own sanity, be prepared.

- Get young toddlers used to the idea of a holiday abroad by pretending to take little holidays beforehand to teach them what the journey will be like – and how you expect them to behave.

- It may be called a 'travel system', but your three-in-one pushchair/car seat/pram is the last thing you need at an airport. Instead check in and use a lightweight fold-up buggy that you can leave at the aeroplane door.

- For me, the most challenging moment of air travel has to be getting through security with children in tow. Remember you are likely to be juggling armfuls of coats and hand luggage – and on top of that, tighter rules mean that the whole family will have to take their shoes off. You will then have about thirty seconds to get them all back on again. So avoid trainers like the plague and choose slip-on shoes for you and your children. For kids getting on planes, I always think Ugg-style boots or Croc-style sandals are perfect.

- Take as little liquid and baby food as possible through airport security if you don't want the stress of proving your baby food jars and bottles don't contain explosives. Remember anything over 100 millilitres is likely to be confiscated – and that's not much. The good news is that most major airports will have a chemist shop stocked with baby food on the other side of security, but go on to the airport's website to check first. Travel with baby-friendly airlines that provide warmed baby food once on board – or make it simple for yourself by mashing up whatever you get served on board with some milk.

- Look for direct or non-stop flights. They may cost more, but avoiding the stress of connecting journeys will be worth it. Take night flights whenever possible.

- Kids can get fidgety and bored before you even take off. So if you are travelling with someone, let them take advantage of the invitation to board first – and load the hand luggage on – while you keep the kids entertained at the gate until the last moment.

- Have a bottle – or breast – ready for takeoff and landing because the sucking motion helps stop kids' sensitive middle ears from hurting.

- Before you take off, most stuff will need to be packed in the overhead locker, so keep a hard core of essentials – snacks, drinks, wipes and favourite toys – in a small bag you can tuck under the seat in front.

- Get your seats assigned in advance if possible so you can bag the bulkhead. As well as good for babies, it is useful for young toddlers who can sit up and use it as a play space.

113

● Take lots of novelties to keep kids amused – but don't take fiddly things like Lego or jigsaws that will drop down the sides of the seats. Opt for larger all-in-one toys that don't fall apart, such as scribble pads.

● Bring plenty of wipes. You can never have enough, especially on an aeroplane, where germs are rampant.

● Don't skimp on snacks. Never rely solely on airline food. If the wait for the food trolley seems a long time to you, imagine what it's like for a toddler. Try to pack food that's not too crumbly, salty or likely to melt, such as cream cheese bagels. Buy bottled water in the departure lounge before you board so that the kids get as much as they need without having to wait.

● As well as taking changes of clothes for the kids, dress in layers so you can peel off the old ones to reveal a fresh, clean layer.

● Forget your policy on limiting TV time. Get through as much of the flight as possible by letting kids watch the airline's video channels.

● Load up on disposable bibs so you are not carrying gloop-covered ones in your bag.

Time-savers for Other Special Occasions

Birthdays

Buy a gift wrap holder: Wrapping paper can be fiddly to store, so buy a special upright holder and also use it to keep ribbon, tape, bows and tags. Only buy sticky tape on a dispensing roll so you are not wasting time endlessly trying to find the edge.

Bag it: Better still, instead of wrapping up presents, buy a selection of coloured paper gift bags (although I often buy the cheap brown paper ones and let the kids decorate them). Just slip the gifts inside, and tie the handles together with ribbon.

Buy in bulk: Don't go shopping every time your child has a party. Snap up toys whenever you see them on sale, and bag them all in one go so there's never a last-minute panic. Some of the best deals are often from children's book clubs. For instance, one company recently offered all fifteen Roald Dahl paperbacks for just £15.99 – a saving of nearly £70 – enough to keep a child's class in presents for the rest of the year. There was no membership fee or postage fee either.

Think ahead: Send out a big batch of that month's birthday cards once a month, rather than staggering them over the weeks and having to make repeated visits to the postbox. Just mark the envelope: 'For opening on your birthday'.

Cheat's Tips for Easiest Kids' Parties

These days, there is a huge choice of children's parties offered by play venues and leisure centres. But if your child is younger and you would prefer something more personal, here are some short cuts.

Share the responsibility: Hold a joint birthday party with a friend of your child who has a close birthday. It's half the organization – and the cost.

Limit your guest list: Don't feel you have to invite the whole class if you haven't got space. The golden rule for a manageable number of guests is one per year age of the child. If you're only asking your child's friends, discreetly email their mums, rather than letting your kids distribute invites to the select few at school.

Ask for RSVPs by email: If you're handing out invites, include your email address for the replies. They will be easier to keep track of and it will save you telephone time.

Use the internet: There are also some fantastic e-card party invites available on the web – which are just as fun as traditional cards and take a fraction of the time to send. After the party, don't bother with personalized thank you cards. Write down who gave what, and then email a brief thanks with the party picture.

Cater – cheaply: For slightly larger parties, make your life easier by going to the catering section of one of the big supermarkets, which can provide fresh-cut sandwiches, cupcakes and a personalized birthday cake in one order for a reasonable price.

Get ready: Give yourself more time. Decorate the room, blow up balloons, and lay out what you can the night before. If you cover some things in cling film, they will stay fresh overnight.

Head off food and drink mess: Serve clear drinks, like water or lemonade, to avoid stains. Serve bite-sized foods and simple sandwiches without

complicated fillings, such as Marmite, cheese or ham.
Save time on buttering sandwiches by mixing butter
and Marmite up in a mixer to a smooth paste before
you spread it.

Go with paper: Use paper plates, paper napkins,
recyclable wooden utensils and cups, so all the refuse
can be dumped into a plastic bag afterwards, ready
for recycling. Make it more fun by using stripy red
cardboard popcorn containers and Chinese food take-
out containers.

Go outside: If you are holding a party in the
summer, put up a wallpaper table outside, and cover
it with brown paper. Draw on place mats and place
names with crayons – and let the kids fill in the rest.

Forget party bags: They are administrative
nightmares. Instead, choose one party-themed gift
and hand them out as the kids are leaving.

How to Save Time At Christmas...

Get Santa to come to you: Avoid trudging into
your local town centre and queuing for hours for
the kids to see Santa by hiring your own to come
to your house. A whole host of companies now
offer personalized visits for as little as £15 per child.
Compared to the cost of travel and parking, it will
probably work out cheaper and will certainly be more
memorable.

Compile your Christmas list all year round:
Does your mind go blank when the rest of the family

ask what your kids want? When you're out shopping, keep a memo on your mobile phone when you spot things your kids might like.

Take advantage of gift-wrapping services: Some stores will either do it for you or provide you with the materials for sending packages abroad. One particularly hectic year, I did my entire Christmas shop at IKEA and then took advantage of the reams of brown paper and sticky tape they have on hand near the delivery desk. When I got home, all I had to do was dress up my parcels with ribbon. If you order online, many companies, like Amazon, will also send gifts direct from the website already wrapped.

Keep it plain: Use heavy duty rolls of brown wrapping paper – not the expensive, flimsy, patterned stuff, which will leave you with lots of leftovers you can't do much with. There's more of it for less money; it's easy to control and stick down; and it can be dressed up any way you like.

Choose your Christmas tree carefully: They may cost a bit more, but try to buy a tree with shorter, softer needles that drop less, like the Noble Fir. Whatever happens, water your tree regularly to stop the needles falling everywhere. Easier still, go fake. These days, they can be quite as convincing and almost as stylish as real ones.

Save time on table decorations: If you want to make a bit of an effort for Christmas dinner, but don't have time for the washing and ironing afterwards, buy disposable cotton napkins on a roll.

Christmas cards: Christmas cards can be a major chore for a time-stretched mother at the busiest time of the year. So instead of writing out endless pleasantries, keep it simple. Log on to one of the websites, such as www.bonusprint.com or www.truprint.co.uk, where you can turn your favourite family pictures into postcards. On the other side, print a Christmas message. It will take about ten minutes, and you won't need to stuff envelopes. Don't worry that you haven't written a personal message on every one. The fact that there's a special picture on the front will go a long way. Or, even easier, send Christmas cards by email.

Chapter 6

Taming Your Housework

Tips and cheats to head off mess before it starts, end the drudgery and find time for what really matters

The American humorist Erma Bombeck once wrote: 'Cleaning your house with kids around is like shovelling the sidewalk before it's stopped snowing.'

She was right. Trying to keep the house under control with children around is a relentless, and often thankless, task. As soon as you've got one spadeful out of the way, there's more to pick up.

It's rather an outdated idea in the twenty-first century, but for some reason many mothers still feel they have to keep a perfect house, even with so much else to do. And I don't suppose that men have tried very hard to put them off the idea. Strange, isn't it, that while males have learnt to cook, they still haven't learnt to wipe round the bathroom sink!

But ultimately, don't forget that your children need you more than your shelves need dusting. As long as it's safe and reasonably organized, your home doesn't need to be clean enough for the glove test. Change your viewpoint. Look on tidying your home as a way to make your life easier and keep things running efficiently, not as a test of your worth as a woman.

How to Keep Your House Under Control in Less Time

Choose wipe-clean paint: There are few things that prove you have given up on your home more than kiddie handprints left all over the walls. It feels like it's all downhill from there. So choose gloss or wipe-clean paint, and you can clean them off in an instant. It sounds paradoxical, but white is the easiest colour – because you can touch it up more easily when the paintwork gets chipped.

Fit dimmer switches: Change the mood in an instant by turning down the lights at the end of the day. Low lighting will also camouflage the worst of the remaining mess.

Think hardwood flooring: It's easier and won't stain. Having washable rugs instead of fitted carpets will make cleaning more manageable.

Ban ornaments: Avoid trinkets around your living area as much as possible. They are dust magnets that are fiddly to clean and easy for kids to break. Focus on two or three statement items in your living room – and leave it at that.

Get practical photo frames: Never buy frames where you can only replace the picture if you unscrew the backs. Kids grow quickly, and by the time you've got round to finding the right screwdriver, the baby in the picture frame could easily be in secondary school. Instead, invest in frames where you can simply slide the pictures in and out, or even digital photo frames. Also, avoid silver or brass frames unless you want to add polishing off metal tarnish to your to-do list.

Designate a play area: Even if you don't have much room, find a space in your living area that's just for your kids. Make a child-sized table the hub and install a toy box nearby. Make it their own separate area that doesn't need clearing away for meals or any other activities. Screen it off after the kids have gone to bed if necessary.

Buy attractive toys: If they are going to litter your home, you might as well make sure the playthings are pleasant to look at. Don't spend money on the latest gargantuan plastic wonder toy, which your child will tire of in a matter of weeks. Instead, look for traditional, hand-crafted toys that you don't mind having around.

Ditch the stereos: Save space and your sanity by downloading your CDs onto digital players around the house. That way you have your music – and your kids' favourites – at the touch of the fingertips and no discs to put back in boxes.

Be generous with waste bins: Every room should have one to keep it tidy. Forget wicker or leather. A funky moulded design is the most practical, as kids' bins in particular will need a good rinse now and then.

Cover your sofa: Buy a washable throw for your sofa in a fabric that can be chucked in the washing machine the moment it gets soiled. Again, it sounds mad, but white is the best colour – simply because you can chuck it in the washing machine and bleach out any stains. Leather couches are also back in fashion, and of course they are easy to clean. But road test them thoroughly first for comfort and slide-factor

– and also to check the kids' bare legs won't have to be peeled off them.

Ditch the pot plants: I can't remember the last time I went to someone's home and came away thinking how lovely the plant in the corner looked. Generally they are droopy-looking dust magnets, which also shed leaves. Don't make more dusting, watering and vacuuming work for yourself.

Other Ways to Keep Your Home Under Control

● Tidy up as you go along. Do a quick scan of every room as you leave it to see whether there's something you can take and put back in its proper place. Is there a water glass on the bedside table you could deliver to the kitchen now you are heading down there to make the kids' breakfast? Does your child's favourite soft toy really belong on your bedroom floor – or should it be back on his shelf?

● Donate DVDs that the kids have outgrown to the local library or charity shop. Otherwise you will find yourself endlessly shuffling through them for the ones you want. Be ruthless and throw out discs that have scratches and jumps on them, or you will get called to sort them out every time they skip.

● Get rid of anything in your home that's broken beyond repair. There will be less to fight through when you are trying to keep it clean.

● Get into the habit of putting an item back in the place where it belongs – not near it. So, if you have a dirty plate, put it straight in the dishwasher, not in the sink.

- Leave stuff that's out of place – and needs to be put back – in a safe place in a basket at the bottom of the stairs. Every time you go up, take an item and drop it off in its rightful home.

- Put door hooks wherever you can. Hang them from the inside of cupboards for hats and scarves, dressing gowns and handbags, so they are all out of the way.

How to Keep the Hallway Clean

A disorganized hallway can mean serious delays in leaving the house with kids. After a long day, coming back to a home where you have to fight your way through piles of discarded shoes and bags can be soul-destroying. Here's how to have a hallway that will guarantee you smooth exits – and make you glad to be back.

- Kids dumping coats and shoes the moment they walk in the door is the single biggest cause of disheartening pile-ups. It's essential you have enough hooks, including some placed at their level, so they can hang their things up themselves. Consider fitting a separate hat and scarf rack above the coat hooks. Give as much space to pegs as possible, so coats don't knock each other off. A family of four will need eight hooks at the very least.

- Get a shoe cupboard to give your entrance way an instant makeover. It will also mean you are no longer dashing around the house to find the right pair. Get kids into the habit of depositing their footwear as soon as they come in and changing into slippers.

- Keep two door mats – one for outside the door and the other for inside. They will cut the amount of dust that comes into the house by up to 80 per cent and slash the time you spend vacuuming and sweeping.

- When the weather turns colder, put out a separate basket for each member of the family to deposit gloves, scarves and hats so they don't get mixed up.

- As soon as winter is over, take heavy coats out of circulation and store away out of sight.

- Get a mirror in the hallway to give you confidence that you've got it together as you walk out the door. It will also make the children more likely to take some pride in their appearance and to put their coats on properly.

How to Head Off Mess in the Bathroom...

- Forget soap bars. Buy push-down dispensers of foam soap, because, unlike the gloopy liquid kind that kids will play havoc with, they dispense only a little at a time.

- Buy flip-top toothpaste so you are not constantly replacing the lid the children have left off.

- Remove all the sample-sized hair care products and cosmetics you have amassed so you can get hold of the products that really matter. Put them in your overnight bag instead so you're ready to go.

- Get your children colour-coded toothbrushes, not character ones, to head off exasperated

125

complaints that you've handed them Snow White
instead of Belle by mistake.

● Invest in a toothbrush holder, and get kids into the
habit of putting theirs back straight away. Otherwise
they will get lost in the bottom of mildewy cups or
tangled up on the side of the basin.

● Stop trying to squeeze bath toys into a small-
sized mesh bag. Instead, set aside a plastic
bucket in the corner.

How to Clean the
Bathroom Quicker...

● Keep lots of cleaning wipes in the bathroom
so you can give the sink, bath and floor a
quick wipe whenever you have a spare minute.
Also have a squidgy you would usually use for
windows handy to clean the shower door.

● If your kids are old enough not to need you right
next to them when they're in the bath, use the
time to clean up the sink and loo. The steam
will make it easier to wipe dirt and dried-up
toothpaste off surfaces.

● It's hard not to be embarrassed by those hideous
grey rings that form around the bathtub. They are
mainly caused by the talc content in soap, so switch
to natural brands made with glycerin instead.

● To avoid toilet rolls cluttering up the bathroom,
choose a holder that does not need to be
unscrewed every time to replace the roll. Opt for
the simple rod kind – where you can slip the roll
easily on or off.

How to Save Time Keeping Kids' Rooms Tidy

A child's room is their universe and their most secure place in the world. By showing you care about what they think and making them responsible for it, they're likely to be more interested in keeping their environment tidy. Don't be put off organizing your child's room because you don't have the time. A few hours of work will pay off further down the line, not least because you won't need to nag them so much about keeping it under control.

- Small children like to express their independence by being able to access items and later put them away on their own. So fit low shelves in alcoves. They store more than shop-bought shelf units because they make better use of the space.

- Get a big basket for stuffed toys. Everyone ends up with loads, but it's rare that more than two or three are in favour at any one time. Don't allow them to take up space around kids' rooms unless they are very special to them.

- Keep a spare packet of wipes and paper towels to hand in play areas. An extra dustpan and brush – or, even better, a hand-held vacuum – is always useful for picking up paper scraps and other debris.

- Stay away from wallpaper – unless you enjoy spending time redecorating – because children love ripping bits off. It will also date. Instead, use basic, neutral paint colours on the walls in a wipe-clean texture. That way you can change the look of the room with wall stickers and new pictures as your child grows.

● Buy an umbrella stand to hold long items like bats and racquets so they don't need constant propping up against the wall.

● Install a laundry basket so clothes have somewhere to go right away and don't end up on the floor. Help your child to sort by investing in a basket already split into three compartments – for lights, darks and coloureds.

● For big foldable items like jumpers and T-shirts, don't force them into fiddly child-sized chests of drawers. Instead, use medium see-through crates so they can see what's in there, fold clothes away easily and roll them in and out.

● Put shoeboxes without lids in drawers to use as compartments to keep clothes from getting jumbled. Put socks in one shoebox, pants in the next.

How to Get Kids to Help

● Praise younger children for trying, not for results. At this stage, you are getting them to feel good about tidying up, not making them into industrial cleaners.

● With older children, don't just march into their rooms and shout: 'Tidy your room!' or they'll just switch off. Instead, get them on their way by setting a couple of specific tasks, like picking up clothes and making the bed. Make it feel more fun and manageable by giving them a 10-minute time limit – and let them do it to music if it moves them along.

- If kids share rooms, stop blame games about who didn't put away what by colour-coding property with stickers. Mark each child's own space with rugs and use barriers, like bookcases, to give them privacy.

- Give children a fighting chance by allocating a place for everything. Use tie racks for hair accessories, ice cube trays for marbles and rock collections, and cutlery trays and tool boxes for pens and paints.

Staying on Top of Paperwork

- Create photo albums online: I know several quite experienced mums who haven't even got around to putting their wedding pictures in an album, let alone their children's baby pictures. The problem is that eventually the task becomes so gargantuan they just can't face it. Even if you can't face the backlog, find a photo service which automatically organizes your latest pictures into proper photo books.

- Text your babysitter the moment you get an invite you want to go to. In fact, write down every date – along with contact details for the organizer – as soon as you get it.

- Invest in one of those ultra-slim filing cabinets that fit snugly into any corner. They are usually just 23 centimetres across, enough to lay A4 paper flat, and have six drawers to keep paperwork separated and organized. They are also fantastic for helping kids file homework.

● Keep work stuff away from home stuff. Don't let permission forms for a school trip next week get stuck among the tax forms you don't need to look at until next year.

● Don't allow paperwork to build up because you are worried it's not safe to throw it in the bin. Take a pair of scissors to any address and account details. Or stow a hand-held shredder – safely out of reach – close to where you go through your mail.

● Pay everything by direct debit. It's generally cheaper. Get online banking and arrange for text alerts to be sent daily to your phone so you can keep a close eye on your account.

● Use postcards as thank-you notes. You won't have to track down and stuff envelopes – and, even better, you won't have to dream up loads of things to write because there's no space.

● Only touch each piece of paper once. Try to deal with it then and there. When you sort through mail, immediately throw it away if it's rubbish and discard envelopes.

● We all get inundated with catalogues – but the right one can be a busy mum's best friend. Try to go through them only once, marking the products that interest you with a pen. Religiously throw out any that are out of date.

● Ask your school Parent Teacher Association to compile the addresses, mobile phone numbers and emails of all the mums in your kids' classes to help organize play dates and school pick-ups.

● Keep a secret set of spare keys for those days when you really can't find them in a rush. Also give a set to a trusted neighbour or friend who lives nearby. With so many things to think about when you leave the house with children, it's inevitable that one day you will lock yourself out.

● Get friendly with your postman. He's more than a delivery man; he's your interface with the outside world. Now you're likely to be shopping more online, there's nothing more irritating than narrowly missing a drop-off – and then having to trudge to the post office collection point and stand in a queue to collect it. Chat to your postie and tell him where he can leave parcels that are too big to fit through the letter box. Explain that it also might take you longer to get to the door sometimes because you've got kids, and ask him to knock a couple of times before he gives up.

● Try to avoid printing out documents that will add to a paper mountain. If you can get email on your phone, send vital documents to yourself, so you can have them to hand.

● Get a phone with a headset or get a shoulder rest. Okay, you'll feel like an idiot to start off with. But this way you can do mindless tasks, like unloading the dishwasher and hanging up the washing, with both hands while you chat.

● If you're working on your laptop around kids, put your computer on a book or a slightly higher surface in case the kids knock any liquid over, to give you a few seconds' grace.

● Keep a master to-do list. When your head is spinning in every direction, it's essential that you write down what needs to be done. Keep it going on your the notepad feature on your mobile so you can add to it wherever you are.

● Organize everything you save to the computer to do with the children with the word 'KIDS' first in the catch-line – so you don't have to fish around for documents.

The Things You Can Never Have Too Much of Around the House

Scissors

Sticky tape

Zip-lock bags

Baby wipes

Household cleansing wipes

Batteries

Stamps

Blu-tack/whitetack

PART II

The Hassled Mum's Guide to Looking Good, Keeping Fit and Feeling Great

Chapter 7

How to look just as good but in a fraction of the time

There was a time when as soon as you had kids, you could stop bothering about the way you looked. By the time you were thirty-five, it was fine to look comfortably mumsy, let the weight pile on and get a Mrs Merton perm. These days, however, we mothers are expected be every bit as glamorous as we were before we had the kids – but without the luxury of hours in the day to do it.

Not surprisingly, in a recent survey of mums, more than 70 per cent said they felt their appearance had suffered as a result of having children. How fondly I look back on the days when I could spend two hours getting ready to go out, get a facial every weekend and blow-dry my hair. When I had my first baby, Lily, grooming was the first thing to go. I dreaded washing my hair. By the time I had shampooed, rinsed, conditioned and tried to get a comb through my alarming-looking bird's nest, my time was up. Lily was yelling, and frankly I wanted to scream too. On Saturday mornings, when I tried to catch up on the essentials like shaving my legs, within half an hour my sleep-deprived husband would be banging on the bathroom door, begging for relief from an unreasonable toddler.

Then there were the *Supermarket Sweep*-style shopping raids where I would attempt to restock my wardrobe. I would charge through clothes rails with my Maclaren, often buying anything in sight. I had to hope it would fit because there was no chance of Lily ever giving me the chance to try it on. Gradually I no longer bore any resemblance to the woman my husband had once married. The only look he ever saw me wear was one of sallow, un-made-up self-pity.

But it began to hit home how badly I had let things slide when I started deliberately turning up late for nursery so none of the mums would see me with messy hair and no make-up. Finally, when a friend told me her husband said I reminded him of one of the Desperate Housewives – not a glam Teri Hatcher but a harassed Felicity Huffman – I got angry.

Then I got groomed. I went back to the beauty basics, interviewed experts and found out how to streamline my old routine. So, after pulling myself out of my slump, I am here to tell you that looking frumpy and neglected does not make you a better parent. You are not being noble by sacrificing your appearance to the cause of motherhood. Just remember that making yourself feel good also makes you a better mother. So here's how to look just as glam – but in half the time.

The Fast Mum's Face: The Rules

Buy make-up that does more than one job: Look for products that do two, or even three, things at the same time. For example, buy mascara that both curls and lengthens to avoid having to fiddle around with an eyelash curler. Or try gels that double as lip glosses, and combined foundation and powder compacts.

Cut out the middleman: Once upon a time, you probably had a vast array of make-up brushes for every conceivable job. Now you don't have the time to find them, let alone wash them. So choose make-up with built-in applicators like lip gloss and concealer pens. Or easier still, plump for make-up you can put on with your fingers, like tinted moisturizers and gel blushes, which are more natural looking anyway.

Use a make-up primer: It may sound strange to add one extra step before you've even started, but use a primer. It's quick, fills in surface imperfections like large pores and lines, and you can apply it without looking in the mirror (always a good test of a mummy-friendly make-up technique). Primers also help make-up to last longer – so you will have fewer of those depressing 'God, I look a state, don't I?' moments later in the day.

If in doubt, chuck it out: Life is so much simpler when you edit out the stuff you don't need. It doesn't matter what make it is, having make-up you don't use hanging around is a waste of space. Apply the wardrobe rule: if you haven't worn it for a year, bin it.

Keep two sets of make-up – and never, ever mix them up: Put one set in your handbag in a clear bag so you can see what's in there and get to it fast. Then leave it there – never to be removed. At the very least, make sure you keep a combination rouge/lip gloss in your wallet to revive you in times of need.

Do your make-up on the move: Get a professional make-up artist's make-up box to help keep it all beautifully organized. Take it wherever your kids are. If they are happy playing with blocks in the playroom, take your kit there too – and you may get to mascara a few extra lashes.

Save the bigger grooming jobs for night time: The mornings are hectic enough, so just use them for putting on make-up. When the kids have gone to bed, take time to bleach your moustache, paint your nails or pluck your eyebrows. Or take advantage of bath time with the kids and put on a mud mask for a Shrek impersonation.

Buy make-up that looks after itself: Wind-up pencil applicators aren't great value for money, because there's not much product in there. But there is nothing more irritating than not being able to find a liner with a sharp tip at the bottom of your make-up bag. So on this occasion, take convenience over price!

Think about packaging: When you are looking for moisturizers and foundations, search out products that are easily dispensable, either by pumps or aerosols rather than jars or tubes. That way, it won't be quite such a disaster if you can't find the top, and they are less likely to dry up or spill.

Choose a tinted moisturizer over foundation: Tinted moisturizer is another of those beauty aids that passes the big test of mummy-friendly make-up. It does three things at once: gives coverage, moisturizes and offers sun protection. Look for a product with light-defusing particles to brighten up your skin.

Go for shades as close as possible to your natural colours: When you are trying to look good in the minimum time, don't experiment. Bright tones will only underline the fact that you could do with some more sleep or a facial. Applying a statement shade of deep scarlet lipstick is going to take an awful lot more time and concentration than a subtle lip gloss close to your own lip colour. Steer clear of orange or toffee-coloured lipsticks too, which can be ageing.

Eye-whitener/red-eye drops: Trust me – after working late or a sleepless night, this is the ultimate beauty secret for the hassled mum. You will look fresh as a daisy – even before you've applied a scrap of make-up.

Nail short cuts: For many manic mums, manicured and long polished nails are a distant memory. Still, if you want polished nails for a special occasion, try the new nail pens in a neutral colour. They should dry in seconds. But as with make-up, try to stick to a colour close to your natural shade, so your nails don't look so bad when they get chipped.

Keep it tidy: To keep your dressing table functioning as efficiently as possible, stick a large magnet on the wall to hold must-haves like tweezers, nail scissors and safety pins, plus a needle and thread for emergency clothes repairs. Keep a bin close too for old Q-tips, packaging and make-up wipes.

The Fast Mum's Make-up Bag – The Essentials

Primer to even out uneven skin tone and keep your make-up on for longer

Tinted moisturizer with a built-in sunscreen

Self-curling mascara

Gel blush

A self-sharpening eye pencil

A nude liner and pale lip gloss close to your natural lip colour

A generous-sized make-up mirror

A Powder compact

Speed Make-up: The Ninety-Second Make-up Routine

1. Rather than using a liquid foundation, save time by using an all-in-one foundation/powder or tinted moisturizer that you can apply with your fingers.
Time spent: 10 seconds

2. Instead of using brushes, use a cheek-lip colour that you can put on with your fingers. Keep the product on standby to use on your lips for a more coordinated look.
Time spent: 10 seconds

3. Use a concealer to correct imperfections and as an eye base to open up your eyes. Then use a wind-up convertible eye pencil to emphasize the outer rims.
Time spent: 20 seconds

4. Save time curling lashes by using a mascara that also curls, such as Maybelline Wonder Curl.
Time spent: 30 seconds

5. Apply a lip-liner, and then quickly fill it in with a two-in-one lip glaze that colours and shines.
Time spent: 10 seconds

6. Blot out any shine with powder.
Time spent: 10 seconds

Things to Do Now That Will Save You Time in the Long Run

Dye your eyelashes: This is a brilliant thing to do about once a month. Waking up and looking like you already have mascara on gives you an instant lift, and saves so much time applying and removing the real thing.

Get your eyebrows shaped: Like many women, I agonized for years about what shape my eyebrows should be – and at one stage I over-plucked them so much they looked like two inverted commas. Stop wasting time trying to get it right. Go to a professional to get the correct basic shape. It will take ten minutes and will make you look younger and less tired. Then carry your tweezers with you wherever you go, and pluck stray hairs as soon as they appear. It's the easiest way to make your face look groomed without even the tiniest scrap of make-up.

Rinse your hair in cool water: Hate the bird's nest look when you get out of the shower? For the last two minutes let the water run cool. Your hair will be easier to comb through and shinier. You can also make your hair smoother by putting your hair dryer on cold.

Sleep with your conditioner: Go to bed slathered in the stuff and covered with a shower cap. Your hair will be healthier, less frizzy and easier to style for the whole week.

Mix your products: Mix your sunscreen with your moisturizer, or your exfoliator with your cleanser and get the job done in half the time.

Get down to basics: I am sure there were times when you could religiously do a five-step skin-cleansing regime every night and had different potions for your neck and under-eye areas. The likelihood is those times are now gone. Toner feels nice, but do you really need it? Instead, cut back your regime to the bone with a good face wash, a flannel and a moisturizer.

Keep a spare bag of make-up wipes: You already know I swear by wipes of every kind, and my make-up table is no exception. Keep a packet of wipes for wiping up spills, cleaning up dispensers, freshening up your face before touch-ups and for nights when you are too knackered to take off your eye make-up properly.

The Hassled Mum's Quick Cheats for Looking Glam...

Wear sunglasses: They hide bags, lack of mascara and can even help sort out bad hair days. The bigger the lenses the better. They're fantastic for making you feel glamorous on the most unglamorous of days.

High ponytails: It works for Kate Moss when she hasn't had time to wash her hair, so why not you?

Pretty shoes: Just because you can't wear stilettos doesn't mean you have to wear trainers all day long and feel dumpy. Look for something in between. You can still get away with a one-inch heel after all.

Get it delivered: Don't run out of essential beauty products that are key to your look. Work out which products you replace all the time, and track them down on a website.

The Hassled Mum's Guide to Getting Your Hair Under Control

Unless you're prepared to live with a crew-cut, your hair is probably the hardest beauty task of all to master as a busy mother. Some of my more stressful moments have been with children clinging to my legs for attention, while I endeavoured to persuade my frizzy cowlicks at the front to go poker straight to make myself feel like me again.

So I gave up fighting my wavy hair and took the low-maintenance route. Take another look at how you are handling the three big Cs – condition, cut and colour – and you may find a way to liberate yourself.

Condition: Whatever your hair is like, try to cut back on the blow-dry habit. Maybe you are caught in a vicious circle: in an effort to get the job done quickly, you dry your hair on the high heat setting, and your hair has become drier and frizzier. You then have to blow-dry it even more to tame it.

But if you take a few steps to get your hair back into condition, you will be able to wean yourself off this particularly time-draining addiction. Try going cold turkey, or at least put the setting on cold. To give it a super quick burst of shine, rinse in cool water. It will make it glossy and encourage you to get out of the shower quicker on school-run mornings.

Cut: Some mums will do it, but I don't think it's realistic for women who seduced their partners with Rapunzel-like locks to chop them off the second they have children. Your man most likely won't appreciate your new 'practical' look.

Even if you cut it off, it will still need lots of styling to make it look good. And at least if it's longish, you can quickly throw it back into a ponytail. But do get your hairdresser to make whatever kind of hair you have more manageable. Have a consultation with your stylist as soon as you sit down so they know what your hair really looks like – not when it's been washed and combed. In real life, they've not there every day to blow-dry your hair. Then tell him or her you need a cut that suits your hair – and that won't need blow-drying to maintain. Don't have short layers if your wavy hair means you have to tease it straight every time you wash it. Instead, work with it. And if you have curly or wavy hair, surrender.

Colour: Try to wean yourself off the hair dye. Stay within two shades of your natural colour to ward off obvious roots and lengthen the time between visits to the salon. No one is saying you have to go back to English Mouse. But if you do have block colour, try shifting over to highlights. If you have highlights, try to keep them in your colour range. Make it look as if you've had a fortnight in the sun, not that you've changed your identity. You may be surprised by how much better you look. Having had red, black and blonde hair in my time, it took me twenty years to realize the most flattering colour for me was just a few shades lighter than my naturally chestnut-coloured hair.

Fast Hair Tricks For
Busy Mothers

Get the right equipment: Invest in a powerful hairdryer – between 1,500 and 1,700 watts with an ionizer. Ionizers work by making the water drops in your hair even smaller, helping to dry your hair faster.

Get speedy products: Check out new blow-drying products which promise to speed up the process.

Target the most obvious sections: If you literally only have a few minutes, dry only the top and the front. Start at the crown first so you are not brushing moisture down into the rest of your hair. Then concentrate on the bits at the front, which is the only part people really look at. Make sure you use the nozzle attachment too; it directs and condenses the air flow.

Dry shampoo: For those days when you know washing your hair will make you late, there's always dry shampoo. If you have long hair, the night before put it in a plait and then into a bun. When you undo it the next day, the wave should have returned to your mane. Then tip your head upside down and spray the crown with a dry shampoo – and you will hopefully find you have a Sienna Miller-style mass of loose, glossy waves.

How to Wake Up Looking
Radiant... Even When
You're Exhausted

If you are a mum under pressure, surviving on not very much sleep, there will no doubt be mornings when you are almost too afraid to look in the mirror. We've all been there. But there are some ways to ensure you jump out of bed looking almost ready for the day. Best of all, you can do them last thing at night, when you finally have some time to yourself.

- Put your hair in a ponytail when you go to bed. That way it stands a better chance of looking reasonably grunge and knot free in the morning.

- Apply fake tan last thing at night with your moisturizer – whatever the weather. You will wake up looking healthy and glowing and needing loads less make-up.

- Make sure you take off all your eye make-up before bed, so your eyes aren't bloodshot or irritated.

- Drink a glass of water and prop pillows up while you sleep to head off any puffy eyes.

- Splash your face in a sink of ice-cold water to get your glow back.

Chapter 8

Dressing Without the Stress

How to dress yourself in two minutes instead of ten – and still look stylish

There will be some days when you have literally five seconds to get dressed – at most. Here's all you need to know to keep yourself looking stylish in a fraction of the time.

Style Basics For Hassled Mums

Get your colours done: Take the guesswork – and the tangerine and lilac wardrobe mistakes – out of your wardrobe. When you actually know for certain what colours work with your hair and skin, you will be able to go into any shop and instantly identify the items that are right for you. It means you will also end up building a wardrobe of matching colours that will take the time-wasting indecision out of shopping. It will also make it easier and faster to shop online.

Get out a tape measure: Do you actually know what your measurements are – or do you usually make an educated guess? When you're shopping on the internet, be equipped with all your vital stats – including the length of your legs – to save on returning items that don't quite fit.

Check it out online first: If it's an emergency and you have to head for the high street, spend half an hour browsing through the collections online first so you have an idea of what's out there.

Try denim: Whether it's jeans or a skirt, look for a dark colour. Remember that muffin tops are only good in bakeries, so ditch the ultra-low hipsters. Otherwise jeans should be a classic style (so boot-cut or straight leg preferably). They also need to fit well and be long enough to wear with heels, but not so long that you can't wear them with trainers or flats.

Invest in good underwear: If you have grey bra straps, droopy bras that have lost their lift, saggy pants, underwear that can be seen when it's not meant to be, then you will look – and feel – like a slob. Get your bust size measured, in case it's changed since having kids, then restock. If your mummy tummy won't go away, invest in some good control pants to hide the jelly belly underneath. Keep them only for special occasions though, as they can be a nightmare to peel on and off.

Get help: If you have a big occasion coming up and you are out of your glamour groove, consider saving time by getting a personal shopper. Tell them your budget up front. The service is usually free, so it should save you time and money. Some high street stores have even started sending out personal shoppers to your home with the latest collections if you can get enough mums together to make it worth their while.

Find the perfect dress shape for you: Find a style that flatters, then look for it in materials that wash well. Beware of too many zips and buttons. If possible, it should slide over the head in one easy move. When you're trying it on, don't just judge it on how it looks. Time how long it takes to put on and consider whether it will need ironing.

Make it easy: Forget the clothes that need special care or say 'dry clean only'. Say goodbye to silk, sequins, beads, bows that untie and the rest. Resist bell sleeves, ribbons or ties that will end up trailing in all sorts of unspeakable substances. Steer clear of stripes or spots. Bold prints will be impossible to match with tights and other accessories in a rush.

Check the return policies: Find a couple of internet sites where you feel you know the clothes suit you – and that also have reasonable return policies. Also consider websites like ASOS where the clothes are modelled on screen so you get an idea of how the outfits look on.

Layer it: Wear layers you can peel off as they get progressively covered in sick, paint, baby food and so on.

Buy longer tops: Unless you are very lucky, your tummy probably isn't as flat as it used to be. So dump short tops. There's nothing more uncomfortable than continually tugging them down over a bulging stomach.

Wardrobe Tips For Mums in a Rush

● If you have the room, hanging is easier than folding and you can see what you've got more easily.

● Throw out wire hangers as soon as they enter your house. You will only end up wrestling with them when they get tangled up in your wardrobe.

● Invest in decent wooden hangers with rubber ends or clips so you are not constantly re-hanging clothes that have slipped off.

● You won't be going anywhere, I hope, without your underwear. Yet there have been many mornings when I have been hunting around in the tangled mess of tights, belts and bras to find a pair of pants. Get some plastic dividers – or even shoeboxes – to divide up your drawers.

● Keep your tights separate from your socks, and as soon as the weather is warm enough, banish them from your sight before they create any more chaos.

The Perfect Hassled Mum's School Run Dress

● Is machine washable

● Layers well

● Doesn't have elaborate zips, buttons and other fastenings

● Skims your body but doesn't squeeze it

- Shows off your thinnest bits and hides your fattest bits

- Doesn't need ironing

- Goes over jeans/leggings and long-sleeved T-shirts and polo necks when the weather gets colder

- Has no hanging long sleeves, bows or ties

- Has an attractive neckline

- If you're breastfeeding, is front opening or has a low-scoop neck

The Hassled Mum's Perfect School Run Wardrobe: The Essentials

- A good, well-made dark coloured coat

- A macintosh for rainy days

- A pair of black leggings to wear with baggy knits and under dresses

- A pair of dark blue jeans: if your stomach just can't be contained, buy a pair with a control panel

- A white shirt to dress up with scarves or down with cardigans and V-necks

- A black polo neck jumper to wear with jeans and under dresses

- Your signature dress in several different fabrics and colours

- A bad hair day hat

- A set of black and white long-sleeved T-shirts to go under tops and take dresses from summer to winter

❀ A pair of knee-length boots with a solid heel

❀ A pair of Converse trainers

❀ A pair of ballet flats.

The Perfect School Run Coat

Because of the delights of the British weather, your coat is always going to be a key item in your wardrobe – so it's important to get it right. A good one will also hide all manner of sins underneath – pyjamas if necessary – and still make you look pulled together.

❀ Look for a dark, plain colour – preferably black, brown, grey or navy – that will wear well and won't need repeated dry-cleaning. If it sounds dull, you can always accessorize or brighten it up with scarves if you ever get a spare minute.

❀ Choose a smart, but not too tight, shape – so it can be slipped over most things without a struggle but doesn't look like a shapeless sack either. A-line often works well.

❀ Make sure it's lined for warmth – and buttons up high if necessary. It should also hang below the knee so it meets the tops of your boots.

❀ If your style will allow it, look for a coat with a hood. That way you won't need an umbrella when it starts raining – and will have a spare pair of hands for the kids.

❀ Consider buying one with large square pockets – to carry all manner of things from your child's breakfast snacks to baby bottles and of course your keys and mobile phone. A good-sized pair of secure pockets will also give you the freedom to leave the house without a handbag if you're in a real rush. Beware of pokey triangular pockets. Everything will just fall out before you've even realized it.

A Final Word About the Busy Mum's Perfect Boot

Boots are a hassled mum's best friend. A comfortable pair of knee-highs can make you look more put together and head off the need for fiddly tights or self-tan pasty legs. They should also enable you to wear virtually any skirt in your wardrobe. So here's a quick guide on what to look for when choosing this staple piece of footwear.

- Choose a pair that can be slipped on and off in an instant. Avoid zips, which can snag tights and calves when you are in a rush. Steer clear of time-consuming laces and buckles.

- Of course you can slip Ugg boots on and off in a flash, but be careful to team them with a slim leg, unless you want to look like a Cossack.

- Avoid kitten heels, which don't give enough support when carrying little ones or sprinting to the school gates. The wear and tear on the tiny surface area will also mean they will constantly need to be constantly re-heeled.

- Look for a solid, square heel that gives you a flattering inch or two of lift off the ground but also the support you need. To make them more slip-proof, make sure they have serrated soles.

- Forget about ankle boots or short boots. You won't have time to coordinate with tights.

The Hassled Mum's Perfect Handbag

A good handbag is the control room of the busy mum's life. Getting under control can mean the difference between feeling prepared to face the world and scarcely daring to leave the house.

Design

- Get a size that's not so small that it's constantly overflowing but not so big you need wheels to pull it along.

- With a larger bag, check that the straps are a comfortable width so they won't dig into you. Ideally it should have a handle long enough for it to go over your shoulder but short enough to carry from the elbow, so you have a spare hand for a child if needs be.

- Avoid bags in soft, light-coloured leathers that stain easily. Instead opt for darker, harder materials – or even wipe-clean patent! But if possible, try to avoid bags with black inner linings. They will make it hard to find anything in a hurry.

- When you are shopping for a new bag, try it with the coat you will usually wear with it so you know it will fit comfortably over your arm. Equally for summer, make sure the material is not too hard against bare skin.

- At the shop, don't just go on how a bag looks when stuffed full of nice light tissue paper. Put your old bag inside to see how it looks when it's fuller.

● Make sure when you put the bag down, it stands up. The last thing you want is to put it down and find the entire contents spilling out onto the floor.

● Check it's got the right number of compartments and outer pockets that close securely. It should have sections for your purse, mobile phone, keys, lipstick and sunglasses and, if possible, something at the end to hold a bottle or beaker upright. Don't overdo it, though. I once bought a bag with five pockets on each side. Finding my mobile was like playing treasure hunt.

How to Manage the Contents

● You are going to need to fit everything inside it, bar the kitchen sink, so shrink everything down. Buy a mini brush and travel-sized versions of your favourite make-up.

● Do you feel that you are constantly fishing around in your bag for your mobile, which only rings for five seconds before it goes to voicemail? I sometimes wonder whether it's a ruse by phone firms to get you to make more calls. However, it's a little known fact that you can ask your provider to text you a code, which will allow it to ring for longer and give you a fighting chance of answering it.

● Get into the habit of always putting your mobile in the same zippable outer pocket every time, so you are not constantly rooting around in a panic for it. Keep it away from anything wet if you want it to survive.

● Store nappies and wipes in separate zip-lock bags. Otherwise the wipes will either dry up or leak, and the nappies will swell up when they get moist.

● Spare yourself the experience of finding your baby's congealed bibs in your handbag. Instead, buy some bib clips. When you're out, it means you can clip any napkin or handy tea towel around your baby's neck, giving you an instant cover-up you can leave at the scene of the crime. They save loads of space in your bag too – and stop it turning into a grubby cesspit.

● Only keep ballpoint pens in your bag. Pencil leads will break. Felt-tip or roller-ball pens will at some point meet with your baby wipes or bottle and start a nightmarish chromatography experiment.

● If you keep a small pocket diary, make sure it has a waterproof cover, and again only write using a biro, so all the writing doesn't run if it gets wet.

● Buy the most substantial key ring you can find to make keys harder to lose. Don't bother with the type that beep when you whistle. I thought it would change my life, only to find out the alarm was set off by every screech and cry. Instead, consider using a long bendy wire or a bright-coloured ribbon to attach your keys to your bag handle, so you can always fish them out from the depths.

● Never be tempted – even in a hurried moment – to put any food in your bag unless it's in some sort of sealed container. Otherwise you will soon end up fishing out oatcake fragments, squashed satsumas – and much worse. Even the firmest, ripest banana can cause havoc in seconds if forgotten in the bottom of a handbag. Get a bag clip to seal half-eaten packets of snacks too.

● When it comes to your period, don't put paper-wrapped applicator tampons in your bag. Inevitably they will come into contact with some sort of wetness, swell up and burst out of the wrapper, making them unusable. By comparison, the bullet-shaped plastic-covered ones stay dry and are more compact.

● Keep your extra set of make-up (remember your duplicate copy that you supposedly never remove) in a tough clear plastic bag with good zips, like the ones they sell in airports. That way you will be able to see the product you need instantly, rather than have to root around for it.

● If you are out and about with your child, take some entertainment. Buy everything in miniature, like mini colouring books, pencil sets and even tiny plastic doodle pads. They don't take up much room, but on a trip out of the house they can make all the difference. The perfect handbag-sized entertainment is the 'Red Fox Mini Treasures' range of children's book – which are miniaturized versions of favourites like *The Runaway Train* and *Avocado Baby* at just a fraction of the price.

● Remember: If disaster does strike with your favourite bag, it can be saved. Even leather ones can be salvaged by a good dry-cleaners.

A Few Words About Keeping Your Bag Safe

The hard, cold fact is that handbag snatchers just love distracted mothers. While you've got a screaming or wandering child to deal with, it's so easy to forget your bag is now being eyed up by a sharp-eyed thief. It's happened to several of my mother friends, and it's one thing that can really ruin your day. Here's how to keep it safe:

- When you are choosing your bag, make sure it closes securely, including the outside pockets.

- If your pram has a horizontal bar for pushing, invest in a secure, heavy-duty handbag clip, or use a curtain ring that shuts, not just a hook.

- Keep your baby facing towards you in the pram for as long as possible, so you don't need to go round – and away from your valuables – to deal with a crying little one.

- If you need both hands free to tend to your baby in a shop, choose a safe spot. Reverse your pram into an inaccessible corner to protect your bag. That way no one can grab it while you're dealing with your little one.

- In cafés and restaurants, don't risk leaving your bag on the floor or the back of the chair where it can easily get stolen. Invest in a handbag clip to affix to the table so it's always off the floor and in your view.

- When getting children out of the car, leave your handbag in the vehicle until the last minute – so it's not vulnerable on the pavement.

Chapter 9

I Want My Body Back...

How to stay slim and stick to a diet, even with kids – and sweeties – around the house

As every mother knows, temptation is never far away when you have kids. With the kitchen cupboard and fridge piled high with treats for your little ones, chocolate, crisps and ice cream can be simply too hard to resist. That's not the only danger. A recent study also found mums end up eating extra at kids' meal times too. More than a third of mothers clearing up after tea don't throw away leftovers – but scoff the lot themselves. It means that with each child she has, a woman's chance of becoming seriously overweight rises by 7 per cent, according to a study by the Duke University Medical Center in the US. So here are some tips and tricks to help busy mums stay in shape – and get your kids eating more healthily into the bargain.

- Start the day with an egg. The protein boost will keep you – and the kids – fuller for longer. Most kids love them boiled. Make it fun by giving them a crayon to draw funny faces on the shell before they eat them.

- Never, ever let your children hear you obsessing about your weight, and try not to use the word 'diet' around them. You will pass on your negative body image. Instead explain that you have decided to eat more healthily – and ask for their support.

● Don't be tempted to finish off the kids' leftovers at tea time. As soon as they've finished, pour washing-up liquid over what's left to stop yourself picking – or just throw it straight in the bin.

● Keep treats in a child-friendly container. You'll be less likely to dip into their treat box if it's emblazoned with kiddie cartoon characters.

● If late-night snacking when the kids are in bed is the problem, brush your teeth after dinner. Once you've cleaned up the kitchen, tell yourself it's off limits for the rest of the evening, and if you fancy a drink, ask your partner to get it.

● 'Kids love to crunch foods – so find some alternatives so your cupboards aren't packed full with tempting bags of crisps,' says life coach and trainer Jo Percival, who specializes in helping mums lose weight. 'Try roasting nuts in the oven, and then sprinkle with some soy sauce. They are delicious and full of good fats.'

● Stick a picture of yourself from the time before you had kids on the fridge to keep you focused. When you feel like cheating, remember nothing tastes as good as feeling slim and fit. Then remind yourself that by eating healthier foods, you are staying active for your kids – as well as setting them a great example.

● Do your food shop online on a full stomach. You'll be less tempted to pick up as many treats, and your children won't be throwing a tantrum if you don't buy the things that catch their eye.

● Sit down and eat a proper meal with your kids. That way, if you are satisfied, you will not be tempted to eat all over again when your partner gets home. You'll also be teaching the kids good social skills.

● Try to break the cycle of giving your children chocolate or sweets to keep them quiet or as a reward. It's likely you will end up buying yourself a treat as well. Buy them stickers or their favourite kids' magazine instead.

● Make healthy eating fun for your kids – and yourself – with lollipop-shaped foods, such as corn on the cob, chicken drumsticks and home-made meat and vegetable kebabs.

● After a hard day of looking after the kids, it's easy to feel as though you deserve sweets or an alcoholic drink to wind down. Head off temptation by keeping a lucky dip box of non-food 'rewards', with options like a face mask, a phone call to one of your favourite people, or half an hour with a magazine.

● Cut out fizzy drinks for the kids and yourself. Make your own lower-calorie pop by diluting orange juice with sparkling water.

● If you must reward your kids with sweets, then do it when you are not at home. That's because you are less likely to want to be seen sharing their chocolate and crisps in public – and you won't have supplies of fattening junk food at home tempting you all day long.

● Find a treat that they love and you hate. I wouldn't mind eating a bar of milk chocolate, but somehow snacking on Smarties or JellyTots just seems too ridiculous.

● Don't be too hard on yourself. If you've had a bad day and have eaten most of your toddler's chocolate, don't use it as an excuse to give up on your diet altogether. There's nothing wrong with a little bit of chocolate. It's hogging the whole family size bag that's the problem.

● If you can, go to bed earlier. With so much to do, it's easy to get into a pattern of turning in at midnight – even though the kids are up at 6.30 a.m. Often we eat for a pick-me-up when we're tired. If you are exhausted and overwhelmed, then your self-control is the first thing to suffer.

How to Exercise – Even with the Kids in Tow

Once you have children, it's not just the sheer relentlessness that's so shocking; it's also the lack of time you have left for yourself. One study estimated that new mothers have just one hour of 'me time' a day. By the time you've had a shower and brushed your hair, that's not long. That lack of personal time is part of the reason why women find it so hard to get their figures back after birth.

Although we so often feel we should be back to our best in weeks like certain celebrities, most of us don't have limitless childcare to enable us to work out with personal trainers. So at the phase of life when you probably need to exercise the most – and are probably dying to get out there and burn a few calories – it's almost impossible to do it. To begin with, your best option is to make sure your baby comes too. Keep breastfeeding for a start. You can burn up to 500 calories a day, although it can also make you ravenously hungry. And if you are lucky enough to have a gym with a crèche nearby, go for it.

When your children are very small, the easiest way to gently get back into the swing of exercise – particularly when you don't feel like exposing your flabbier bits to the world – is to use a fitness DVD at home. If your baby is in the habit of taking a mid-morning nap, for example, make a regular date with your DVD player. There are loads available on Amazon that take you through from pre- to post-pregnancy, before you're ready for the tougher stuff. Interactive computer programs like WiiFit can also get you back on track in areas like yoga, step classes and jogging. It will also act as your own personal trainer by charting your body mass index and weight at the same time.

If you have one child at school still small enough to fit into a child seat, try the school run by bike. By boosting your heart rate first thing in the morning, you'll be kick-starting your metabolism for the rest of the day. The other good news is the extra weight of your youngster will really help firm your thighs and bottom.

Otherwise look for a three-wheel, all-terrain pram, which means you can power-walk and really pound the pavement. A twenty-minute walk to the shops could burn up to 175 calories. If you need an extra boost, join a buggy exercise programme for mums at your nearest park. Go to www.buggyfit.co.uk to see whether there's a class near you. Of course, this only works for as long as your child is young enough to stay put – and if you only have one in tow. After that, change your attitude, and start thinking of a visit to the swings as some valuable exercise time you can share with your children.

Sometimes we make exercise far too much of a mountain. Remember when you were a child and you happily played outdoors? Chances are you adored every second and didn't consider it to be a big chore. Step back into that mindset. By using the play equipment like a gym circuit, you could burn nearly 400 calories in an hour – the same as the average gym session. It's not ideal – and you may prefer to frequent the playground at quieter times – but look on it as something you can all do together. To that end, here's a sample work-out devised by personal trainer and women's fitness specialist Jo Percival. So head for the park, and let your kids be your very own personal fitness trainers!

Playing Catch

This is a great warm-up to get you going. Stand feet apart. Then take the ball in both hands and bend over at the waist until you feel a stretch in the backs of your legs. Hold for a few seconds then chuck the ball back to your child and slowly stand upright again. Don't jerk, and keep your movements smooth.

What muscles will I use? Biceps, triceps, shoulders and back muscles.

How many calories will I burn? Ten minutes will burn 80 calories.

Swings

Push the swing firmly with the palms of your hands and extend your arms fully so you can feel your limbs stretch. Put your hands at the very edge of the swing seat to work all the muscles across the chest like a chest press. But don't get carried away – or your child will end up in the clouds! Strong pecs will give you a lift and more definition and support for the fatty tissues that make up the breasts. Jo says: 'While pushing your child, try to alternate which arm you push away with. Both hands for twenty, then twenty each arm. If you are ready, take it a step further by adding lunges. Step forward and dip as you give each push. Then return to standing position and repeat with the other leg.'

What muscles will I use? This will exercise your chest, upper back and triceps. If you lunge too, you will also be working your buttocks and thighs.

How many calories will I burn? Five minutes will help rid you of your underarm 'bingo wings' and burn 25 calories. Add the lunges and you will burn off an extra 20 calories.

See-saw

A see-saw can provide you with a great resistance exercise for your arms and chest. If your child has a playmate, put both of them on the see-saw. Then stand in front of the central pivot point. Bend over and put a palm on each side of the pivot about 2 feet apart. Do as many pushes as you can. When you get tired, have a quick rest but try to repeat three times. If there is another adult with you, try sitting at opposite ends of the see-saw with your kids on your lap, and send each other up and down to give your thighs and buttocks a work-out. You could also try it without anyone sitting on the other end of the see-saw; simply hold your child on your lap and move up and down for a great leg work-out.

What muscles will I use? Front of shoulders, triceps and chest.

How many calories will I burn? Five minutes of using your arms to balance the see-saw will burn 30 calories. Working out your thighs will burn 50 calories in ten minutes.

Slide

If your child weighs under 25 pounds, do a spot of weightlifting by lifting them to the top of the slide. While they are sliding down, stand on the first rung of the ladder. Hold on for balance and raise up onto the balls of your feet, then slowly lower your heels as far as they can go. Go up and down on your toes to work your calves, remembering to support your back by drawing in your tummy. Repeat as many times as you can before your child comes back round for another turn.

What muscles will I use? Back, bottom and calf muscles. This is also great for getting your lymphatic system working.

How many calories will I burn? Three sets of twelve lifts will burn about 20 calories.

Roundabout

As soon as you have lifted your child on and the roundabout is spinning, jog around the outside and pretend to chase her. Keep jogging until your child is ready to stop – or gets too dizzy!

What muscles will I use? Legs, bottom and back.

How many calories will I burn? Approximately 40 calories in five minutes.

Climbing Frame

Now you are grown up, the horizontal bars are the perfect height for working out your back and arms. First try a chin-up. Put your hands shoulder width apart. Grab the bar above you and hang by your arms, then try to pull your chin up towards the bar as you bend your arms. This will require a lot of strength, so don't be surprised if you can hardly bend your arms at all. Come up as far as you can but don't strain yourself. Do this exercise for a minute, then give yourself a full minute's rest. Next try some leg raises, which work out the abdominal muscles. Hang by your arms, bend your legs and raise your knees towards your body.

What muscles will I use? The large muscles in your back and your abs.

How many calories will I burn? Ten minutes will burn 50 calories.

How to Make the Most of Your Playground Work-out

Warm-up: If your kids are still in the buggy, push them to the park with a gentle jog. If they are older, let them ride their bike or scooter and run alongside.

Keep moving: Treat it like a circuit-training work-out.

Give yourself a morale boost with a pedometer: Jo says: 'As a mum, you spend loads of time running after your kids already. Ten thousand steps a day is a good goal, but chances are you do 5,000 even on a quiet day. A pedometer will help motivate you to be super active every day.'

Play tag for a quick burst of cardio: Studies show short bursts of exercise are the best way to burn fat. This is a great way of extending your work-out once you've been on all the equipment.

Have fun: Use it as a great chance to spend time with your children as well as getting nicely toned.

Other Things You Can Do To Keep Trim

Trampolining: As well as being great fun to do with the kids, trampolining boosts everything from bone density to muscle tone and posture. For the average size woman, it also burns about 200 calories an hour.

Skipping: Skipping improves your heart and lungs fitness and makes bones and muscles strong. It also burns up more calories than any other popular exercise except for fast running. Ten minutes of moderate skipping burns 70 calories.

Hula hooping: According to the American Council on Exercise, you should burn approximately 200 calories if you hula hoop for thirty minutes. It's also great for your posture, your pelvic floor and tightening up your abdominal muscles.

Chapter 10

Give Me Back My Life and My Partner

How to find time for your job, your partner and yourself

Not so long ago, the 'Do I or don't I return to work?' question was a major dilemma for modern mothers. Many women could afford to choose whether they wanted to stay at home or keep earning their own money and hold on to their careers.

But these days, fewer mums have the option to choose. For some women, there is simply no alternative but to work – and it's then that the pressure cooker in your head can really start to whistle. Being a full-time mother and going out to work is like trying to hold down two jobs – and being pulled in two different directions.

One memory I do not treasure was when my six-year-old daughter, lying prostrate on the floor as I tried to fax an interview on the deadline (my email had crashed), screamed: 'You said you'd play with me!' Or, when I was a correspondent based in New York, the voice of the world's least sympathetic (and surprise, surprise childless) boss screaming at me for flying home 3,000 miles to my sick two-year-old daughter after completing an interview in Los Angeles. He argued that I should have ignored the fact that she was parentless and ill on the other side of the country (my husband was on another assignment). Apparently, I should have waited another night until he had woken up in the UK to ask his permission to leave. Shortly afterwards, I resigned.

No wonder that instead of chasing bonuses and pay rises, these days working women seek a much more elusive goal: to work for a company that can help them find a work-life balance. Many companies today offer various options which make it easier for women to work around their kids. So here's a basic guide to some of the options.

The Options for Returning to Work

It used to be that you went to work and worked nine to five – or not at all. But thankfully, the situation has come a long way. If you want to go part time you shouldn't have to worry about losing out on bonuses or pensions, because the law states you should be treated just as favourably as full-time colleagues. Companies also have a legal obligation to consider your request for flexible working – and give good reasons for turning it down. Currently you are entitled to ask for flexible working if your child is under six or you have a disabled child under eighteen, and you've had your job for more than twenty-six weeks, but it looks likely that the right is to be extended in the near future.

> **Flexi-time:** Flexi-time allows you to vary a set number of hours, although there is usually a 'core' time when you have to be at work. If you want to make sure you are available to drop your child at school in the morning, for example, you could ask to work from 10 a.m. to 6 p.m. instead of 9 a.m. to 5

p.m. Or, if you also want to collect your children from school, you could request to work from 10 a.m. to 4 p.m. and skip your lunch break.

Job-sharing: Job-sharing is when a position is split, usually between two people. You may want to do mornings, while a colleague may want to do afternoons, for example. Or you might prefer to do the first half of the week, while your colleague works the second half, although you may need a crossover period so you can hand over the reins. The key is to make sure you share with someone with the same priorities – and whom you work and communicate with well. If you are looking for a job like that or part-time work that might fit better with your schedule, try these websites: www.mumandworking.co.uk and www.workingmums.co.uk.

Term-time working: School holidays can be a major nightmare for many mums. But term-time working may allow you to work full or part time during the school term and to take unpaid leave during the school holidays. Your pay may be averaged out over the year. You could also arrange to work school hours only.

Compressed hours: You could also request to squeeze more hours into fewer days, by giving up lunch breaks or working later, so you earn a day off at home.

The Other Choices

Working from home: You can ask your employer to let you save on the time you spend commuting by working all or some of the week from home. If your company is worried about the cost of setting you up, you can even offer to help cover the costs. But don't go into it imagining the baby playing happily at your feet, while you tap away at your computer in your pyjamas. You will still need proper childcare and a dedicated work area. Make sure you go into the office regularly and keep in touch with colleagues so you are not left out of the loop.

Going it alone: Having a baby may have been just the motivation you needed to be your own boss. You will have to bring the work in, and your income is likely to vary from month to month, but at least you will be in charge. Just make sure you treat it as a proper job.

How to Make Your Job Work for You

Leading employment lawyer Belinda Lester, partner at North London law firm CKFT, herself a mum of two, has these tips for working mums:

● Create the best possible impression before you go on maternity leave – and build up the brownie points. 'It will be difficult when the only thing on your mind is your new baby and bootees. But force yourself to talk about the contribution you are planning to make when you do come back.'

● 'Women are really bad at telling employers how good they are. When you are seeking flexible working terms, sell yourself,' says Belinda. 'Point out your unique skills and why they can't do without you – and how flexible working could benefit them.'

● Before you go, tell your employer you would like to be kept in the loop and, if necessary, attend training days. Mums on maternity leave can agree to work for up to ten days without losing their entitlement to maternity leave or maternity pay. Belinda says: 'If your employer wants to offer them – and you're looking to return to work on more flexible terms – it's a good idea to take them. You are in a position to dictate the terms – so you can say you want to be paid your normal salary for those days. Don't be afraid to ask for the money; people value more the things – and people – they pay for.'

● When asking for flexible working when you return, remind employers that your kids won't be little for ever. There will come a day when you can return to work full time.

● Be creative; there are lots of options when it comes to flexible working. You can agree to give up your lunch break in order to leave earlier, or work different hours on different days. Belinda recommends: 'Use your imagination, and try to work with your employer to find a solution that works for both of you.'

● Men have as much right to request flexible working as women, so see if your partner can change his working hours.

● Stop feeling guilty. 'As long as your children feel loved, they'll be fine,' Belinda says. 'And there's a safe bet they already do if you are reading this book. They may sometimes have to wait for you to get off the phone, but all kids have to learn to be patient. Don't let them make you feel bad about working. There isn't a child on the planet who doesn't want more.'

Tips for Working Mothers

Don't take kids into the office: For all the colleagues who coo, there will be others who will think it proves your priorities lie elsewhere. Even though they probably do, don't remind them.

Don't be bothered by resentment: Of course there will be some people who won't like the fact that you've got more flexible hours or are working part time. Don't take it personally. How colleagues respond will also depend on where they are at in their lives. The twenty-something with a long-term partner who is planning to have kids soon is likely to be a lot more sympathetic than the forty-something who's never found the right man or decided not to have children. Try to shake it off by being as relaxed and professional as possible, and by trying to help them out as much as you can in the time available to you.

Screen your calls: Unnecessarily long phone conversations can really eat into your precious time. So politely tell people at the very start of the conversation how long you've got.

Don't say yes to everything: If you are not sure how to phrase a 'no' to a request, ask to check your diary first. To save offence, explain why you can't do it or suggest someone else who might be able to help.

Don't go into too much detail: You may need to rearrange your schedule for your child's sports day, but your colleagues don't need to know that. But do warn your workmates as far as possible in advance when you will be off – and prepare for it.

Beware of smug mummies: They're the ones who make out they have it all under control and don't know what you are talking about when you're honest about how stressed you are. Some women just have an investment in appearing to be on top of it all. They'd rather die than admit they're not. They've either got so much help in the form of bend-over-backwards parents, nannies and cleaners – or they're simply not trying to do as much as you are. Just smile to yourself – and don't fall for it.

Don't compare: Don't compare yourself with your childless colleagues. Plenty of people who work full time also spend a huge amount of time hanging out at the coffee machine, going on cigarette breaks and socializing. Don't beat yourself up by comparing yourself with full-time mums, either. You probably imagine they are with their children every second of the day playing tea parties. But they're not with their kids 24/7 either. They are probably spending just as much time at the shops, having coffee, chatting to other mums and cleaning up the mess their children have made at home.

How Not to Let Your Child be a BlackBerry Orphan

Sure, it's an essential tool that means you're liberated from the office sooner. But when you're with kids, limit its use as much as possible so they know they are getting your undivided time.

- When you're with your children, put your BlackBerry on silent. The constant chirruping every time an email appears will make both them – and you – tense.

- Explain to the kids that it's not a tool that steals your attention, but something that allows you to spend more time with them.

- Be brutal with spam. The only messages to make it to your BlackBerry should be absolutely essential. Tell people not to forward you mass emails. Unsubscribe to unnecessary newsletters and alerts.

- If the answer is likely to be more than thirty words, wait until you get to your computer to reply.

- Make your Blackberry feel more friendly by letting kids help compose an email to Granny or Daddy at work.

- Never send a message during anything that is important to your kids. Older kids in particular will never forgive you if they see you emailing during a school performance or a sports match.

How to Get More Support from Family and Friends

You are not superwoman. Even with the best will in the world, you cannot do all this on your own. As well as your regular child-carer, you need a support network of people not only to help you out in an emergency, but also to allow you to recharge your batteries once in a while.

Grandparents

Parents can forget very quickly what it's like to work when you've got young children. Your mum may not have worked at all since she had you – or if she did, the long hours culture wasn't so ingrained back then as it is today. But the fact is that throughout most of history children have been brought up by extended families – not just by one exhausted mother.

It may be that grandparents haven't suggested it simply because they feel hesitant about interfering or don't realize how much pressure you are under. They may also not be feeling confident about looking after a young child after a long break and may be worried you may not like their style.

But don't be a martyr. Point out that your child's family doesn't end just with you and your partner. Explain to your parents and your parents-in-law that you have a lot on your plate and that you occasionally need help. Get into good habits from the start – or involve them – so they get some practice. Don't exploit them, but make them feel needed by telling them you would much rather your child was looked after by a family member in an emergency. Suggest they could also improve your parenting by occasionally giving you a break to allow you some time to recharge your batteries!

Neighbours, Friends and Fellow Mums

With baby-sitting fees rising far quicker than general salaries, hiring a baby-sitter can cost a small fortune. Getting organized with a baby-sitting circle is one of the best ways to have a ready-made set of carers on tap – and for no cost. If there isn't one at the school or play group or in your road, start one by asking some of the mums near you for coffee and let it build from there.

The best number is between seven and twelve mums, so that it's a manageable number, and kids always have a familiar face. It helps to have parents who have kids with similar ages so your needs are all roughly the same. Then work out a voucher system. Each time you baby-sit for another member of the circle, you receive a token – and lose one when someone baby-sits for you. Or, if that sounds like too much administration, arrange a more informal set-up among three or four close friends. Then, when your kids reach the age of six and up, you can also start arranging sleep-overs with their best friends, and return the favour by giving the other parents a break a few weeks later.

Make an effort, too, to get friendly with other mums at the school gates. Find two or three other parents in the same boat, and take each other's mobile numbers so that you can all step in and help each other out with school runs.

Your Other Half

If you have to go out to work, don't let your man get away with saying things like: 'I don't change nappies' or 'I can't clean.' He can; he just thinks he still shouldn't have to. If you are taking on a traditionally male role, then there's absolutely no reason why he shouldn't take on some traditionally female jobs too.

- Tell your partner what you want. Have you actually told him what you need, or are you being long-suffering and expecting him to guess?

- If he insists it's not his job, make it clear in the nicest possible way that the whole family is a team working towards a happy, relaxed home, and everyone has to muck in together to make it work.

- Work out each other's strengths and preferences when it comes to housework. I love loading the dishwasher but hate unloading it. So my husband does it while he watches the news.

- Don't criticize everything your partner does. Many men don't attempt 'female' tasks because they think they are not very good at them. By all means give some gentle guidance, but, just as with your kids, give credit for effort!

The Hassled Mum's Guide To Making Time for Your Partner

Many mums and dads feel that if they don't devote all their spare time to their children, then they're not being good parents. But the best gift you can give your kids is a stable relationship – and that demands quality 'couple time'. You've got a lot on your plate, but don't let your relationship come last. It's the bedrock of your family's security.

> **Be inventive:** Most of us are too exhausted to think of anything but sleep by the time we get to bed. So get intimate at unusual times of the day, like in the morning before the kids wake up and during baby

and toddler nap times. Don't feel guilty about letting the children watch TV if it allows you an opportunity to reconnect through sex. If it improves your relationship, it will benefit them in the long run.

Bring the kids: You don't have to leave the kids out to have some romance. In fact, it's good for your kids to see you looking happy and relaxed together. At weekends, get out of the house as a family – even if it's just for a long walk in the park where you can hold hands while the children play. Sometimes all it takes is a change of scenery away from the distractions of home to feel a bit closer as a couple.

Turn off the TV: Television is the ultimate time-waster. You may think you're relaxing together at the end of the day, but instead of focusing on your partner, you're focusing on the screen like a zombie. Unless it's a favourite romantic film or a programme you both adore, talk to each other instead.

Look after the minutes: Even the simplest gestures can add up over the week. When you're busy with work and children, often it's a question of finding mere minutes together rather than hours. A hug in the morning and in the evening all adds up – and still makes you feel close – even if you're not seeing much of each other.

Stay loyal to each other: Do your best to be a united front. Even if you disagree behind closed doors about an issue regarding the kids, don't argue about it in front of your children or it will cause huge resentment between you.

Be spontaneous: An 'I love you' text can take a few seconds to send, but the message shows your partner you're thinking of them. Being spontaneous can mean more than a corny card on Valentine's Day.

Don't generalize: Try never to say 'you always' or 'you never' to your partner. There is nothing more irritating, and just like kids, if men feel 'labelled' they give up trying to change. Be specific about situations you would have liked your partner to handle differently, so at least the criticism is constructive.

Conclusion

It would be a tragedy if you looked back at your kids' childhood and all you remembered was rushing from A to B, bundling your children off to school so you could get to work and drowning in housework. But unless we take stock, in these hectic times there is a danger of that happening.

This book was written to stop the too-much-to-do culture stealing away the best moments of being a mother. Hopefully now you've read it you feel a bit less overwhelmed and more able to cope. I also hope you've discovered some eureka moments to help you streamline your life and cut out irritating frustrations that make a tough job even tougher. If it's enabled you to enjoy playing tea parties with your child – rather than feeling stalked by your laundry pile – then this book has achieved its goal.

Use this book to find as much time for your children as you can. There is no perfectly prepared meal, no freshly ironed outfit or spotless kitchen floor that can replace the hours and minutes you spend with them.